Praise for *The Art of Learning*

"We all remember the portrayal of Josh Waitzkin in *Searching for Bobby Fischer*. He was a very impressive child who continues to impress with *The Art of Learning*. Through a unique set of experiences, Waitzkin has formed an original and outstanding perspective. From chess to Tai Chi, he provides tools that allow all of us to improve ourselves every day."

—Cal Ripken, Jr., 2007 Baseball Hall of Fame Inductee

"Waitzkin's engaging voice and his openness . . . make him a welcome teacher."

—*Publishers Weekly*

"A vibrant and engaging look at the love of learning and the pursuit of excellence."

—*Booklist*

"*The Art of Learning* succeeds on every level, by combining a truly compelling autobiography with profound philosophical and psychological insights, all wrapped in a practical how-to framework. This is a must-read for anyone wishing to achieve that rare combination of success and fulfillment."

—Paul Blease, SVP, Director Team Development & Consulting, Citigroup Smith Barney

"Waitzkin's in-depth look into the mental side of his success in both chess and martial arts is an inspiring and absorbing read. I strongly recommend it for anyone who lives in a world of competition, whether it's sports or business or anywhere else. It's also a great training tool for kids aspiring to reach the pinnacle of their chosen fields."

—Mark Messier, 6-time Stanley Cup Champion

"The title is accurate—at a profound level, it's about real learning from hard conflict rather than from disinterested textbooks."

—Robert Pirsig, author of
Zen and the Art of Motorcycle Maintenance

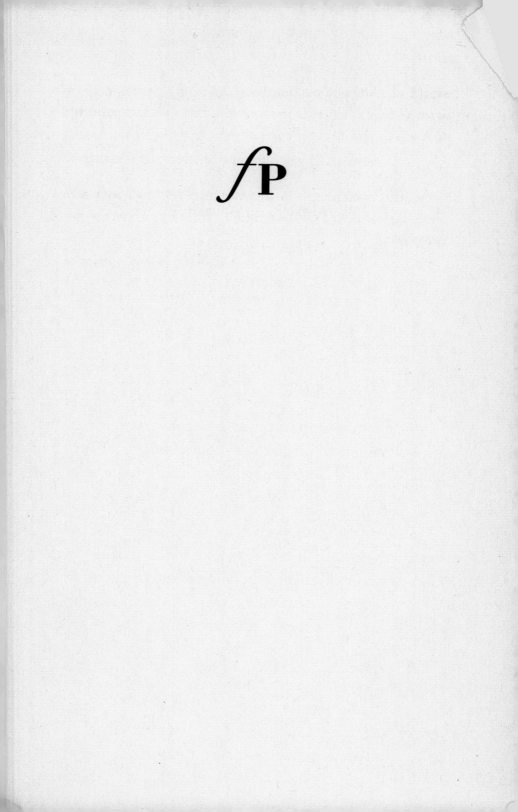

Also by Josh Waitzkin

ATTACKING CHESS

THE ART
OF LEARNING

———◆———

An Inner Journey
to Optimal Performance

Josh Waitzkin

FREE PRESS

New York   London   Toronto   Sydney

FREE PRESS
A Division of Simon & Schuster Inc.
1230 Avenue of the Americas
New York, NY 10020

First Free Press trade paperback edition May 2008

FREE PRESS and colophon are trademarks
of Simon & Schuster, Inc.

Part pages photo credits:
Part 1: Josh at the Manhattan Chess Club, age seven.
Photo by Bonnie Waitzkin.
Part 2: Training for the 2002 Worlds. Photo by Andrew Kist.
Part 3: The second to last throw of the Finals, 2004 World
Championships. Courtesy of the author.

For information about special discounts for bulk purchases,
please contact Simon & Schuster Special Sales:
1-800-456-6798 or business@simonandschuster.com

DESIGNED BY ERICH HOBBING

Manufactured in the United States of America

7   9   10   8

Library of Congress Cataloging-in-Publication Data
Control Number: 2006052539

ISBN 13: 978-0-7432-7745-7
ISBN 10:   0-7432-7745-7
ISBN 13: 978-0-7432-7746-4 (pbk)
ISBN-10:   0-7432-7746-5 (pbk)

For my mom,
my hero,
Bonnie Waitzkin

CONTENTS

III

BRINGING IT ALL TOGETHER

INTRODUCTION

One has to investigate the principle in one thing or one event exhaustively . . . Things and the self are governed by the same principle. If you understand one, you understand the other, for the truth within and the truth without are identical.

—Er Cheng Yishu, 11th century[*]

Finals: Tai Chi Chuan Push Hands World Championships
Hsinchuang Stadium, Taipei, Taiwan
December 5, 2004

Forty seconds before round two, and I'm lying on my back trying to breathe. Pain all through me. Deep breath. Let it go. I won't be able to lift my shoulder tomorrow, it won't heal for over a year, but now it pulses, alive, and I feel the air vibrating around me, the stadium shaking with chants, in Mandarin, not for me. My teammates are kneeling above me, looking worried. They rub my arms, my shoulders, my legs. The bell rings. I hear my dad's voice in the stands,

[*]William Theodore de Bary, *Sources of Chinese Tradition,* Vol. 1, 2nd ed., Columbia University Press, 1999, p. 696.

Introduction

'C'mon Josh!' Gotta get up. I watch my opponent run to the center of the ring. He screams, pounds his chest. The fans explode. They call him Buffalo. Bigger than me, stronger, quick as a cat. But I can take him—if I make it to the middle of the ring without falling over. I have to dig deep, bring it up from somewhere right now. Our wrists touch, the bell rings, and he hits me like a Mack truck.

Who could have guessed it would come to this? Just a few years earlier I had been competing around the world in elite chess tournaments. Since I was eight years old, I had consistently been the highest rated player for my age in the United States, and my life was dominated by competitions and training regimens designed to bring me into peak form for the next national or world championship. I had spent the years between ages fifteen and eighteen in the maelstrom of American media following the release of the film *Searching for Bobby Fischer,* which was based on my dad's book about my early chess life. I was known as America's great young chess player and was told that it was my destiny to follow in the footsteps of immortals like Bobby Fischer and Garry Kasparov, to be world champion.

But there were problems. After the movie came out I couldn't go to a tournament without being surrounded by fans asking for autographs. Instead of focusing on chess positions, I was pulled into the image of myself as a celebrity. Since childhood I had treasured the sublime study of chess, the swim through ever-deepening layers of complexity. I could spend hours at a chessboard and stand up from the experience on fire with insight about chess, basketball, the ocean, psychology, love, art. The game was exhilarating and also spiritually calming. It centered me. Chess was my friend. Then, suddenly, the game became alien and disquieting.

I recall one tournament in Las Vegas: I was a young International Master in a field of a thousand competitors including twenty-six strong Grandmasters from around the world. As an up-and-coming player, I had huge respect for the great sages around me. I had studied their masterpieces for hundreds of hours and was awed by the artistry of these men. Before first-round play began I was seated at my board, deep in thought about my opening preparation, when the public address system announced that the subject of *Searching for Bobby Fischer* was at the event. A tournament director placed a poster of the movie next to my table, and immediately a sea of fans surged around the ropes separating the top boards from the audience. As the games progressed, when I rose to clear my mind young girls gave me their phone numbers and asked me to autograph their stomachs or legs.

This might sound like a dream for a seventeen-year-old boy, and I won't deny enjoying the attention, but professionally it was a nightmare. My game began to unravel. I caught myself thinking about how I looked thinking instead of losing myself in thought. The Grandmasters, my elders, were ignored and scowled at me. Some of them treated me like a pariah. I had won eight national championships and had more fans, public support and recognition than I could dream of, but none of this was helping my search for excellence, let alone for happiness.

At a young age I came to know that there is something profoundly hollow about the nature of fame. I had spent my life devoted to artistic growth and was used to the sweaty-palmed sense of contentment one gets after many hours of intense reflection. This peaceful feeling had nothing to do with external adulation, and I yearned for a return to that innocent, fertile time. I missed just being a student of the game, but there was no escaping the spotlight. I found myself dreading chess, miserable before leaving for tournaments. I played without inspiration and was invited to appear on television shows. I smiled.

Then when I was eighteen years old I stumbled upon a little book called the *Tao Te Ching,* and my life took a turn. I was moved by the book's natural wisdom and I started delving into other Buddhist and Taoist philosophical texts. I recognized that being at the pinnacle in other people's eyes had nothing to do with quality of life, and I was drawn to the potential for inner tranquility.

On October 5, 1998, I walked into William C. C. Chen's Tai Chi Chuan studio in downtown Manhattan and found myself surrounded by peacefully concentrating men and women floating through a choreographed set of movements. I was used to driven chess players cultivating tunnel vision in order to win the big game, but now the focus was on bodily awareness, as if there were some inner bliss that resulted from mindfully moving slowly in strange ways.

I began taking classes and after a few weeks I found myself practicing the meditative movements for hours at home. Given the complicated nature of my chess life, it was beautifully liberating to be learning in an environment in which I was simply one of the beginners—and something felt right about this art. I was amazed by the way my body pulsed with life when flowing through the ancient steps, as if I were tapping into a primal alignment.

My teacher, the world-renowned Grandmaster William C. C. Chen, spent months with me in beginner classes, patiently correcting my movements. In a room with fifteen new students, Chen would look into my eyes from twenty feet away, quietly assume my posture, and relax his elbow a half inch one way or another. I would follow his subtle instruction and suddenly my hand would come alive with throbbing energy as if he had plugged me into a soothing electrical current. His insight into body mechanics seemed magical, but perhaps equally impressive was Chen's humility. Here was a man thought by many to be the greatest living Tai Chi Master in the world, and he patiently taught first-day novices with the same loving attention he gave his senior students.

I learned quickly, and became fascinated with the growth that I was experiencing. Since I was twelve years old I had kept journals of my chess study, making psychological observations along the way—now I was doing the same with Tai Chi.

After about six months of refining my form (the choreographed movements that are the heart of Tai Chi Chuan), Master Chen invited me to join the Push Hands class. This was very exciting, my baby steps toward the martial side of the art. In my first session, my teacher and I stood facing each other, each of us with our right leg forward and the backs of our right wrists touching. He told me to push into him, but when I did he wasn't there anymore. I felt sucked forward, as if by a vacuum. I stumbled and scratched my head. Next, he gently pushed into me and I tried to get out of the way but didn't know where to go. Finally I fell back on old instincts, tried to resist the incoming force, and with barely any contact Chen sent me flying into the air.

Over time, Master Chen taught me the body mechanics of nonresistance. As my training became more vigorous, I learned to dissolve away from attacks while staying rooted to the ground. I found myself calculating less and feeling more, and as I internalized the physical techniques all the little movements of the Tai Chi meditative form started to come alive to me in Push Hands practice. I remember one time, in the middle of a sparring session I sensed a hole in my partner's structure and suddenly he seemed to leap away from me. He looked shocked and told me that he had been pushed away, but he hadn't noticed any explosive movement on my part. I had no idea what to make of this, but slowly I began to realize the martial power of my living room meditation sessions. After thousands of slow-motion, ever-refined repetitions of certain movements, my body could become that shape instinctively. Somehow in Tai Chi the mind needed little physical action to have great physical effect.

This type of learning experience was familiar to me from chess. My whole life I had studied techniques, principles, and theory until they were integrated into the unconscious. From the outside Tai Chi and chess couldn't be more different, but they began to converge in my mind. I started to translate my chess ideas into Tai Chi language, as if the two arts were linked by an essential connecting ground. Every day I noticed more and more similarities, until I began to feel as if I were studying chess when I was studying Tai Chi. Once I was giving a forty-board simultaneous chess exhibition in Memphis and I realized halfway through that I had been playing all the games as Tai Chi. I wasn't calculating with chess notation or thinking about opening variations . . . I was feeling flow, filling space left behind, riding waves like I do at sea or in martial arts. This was wild! *I was winning chess games without playing chess.*

Similarly, I would be in a Push Hands competition and time would seem to slow down enough to allow me to methodically take apart my opponent's structure and uncover his vulnerability, as in a chess game. My fascination with consciousness, study of chess and Tai Chi, love for literature and the ocean, for meditation and philosophy, all coalesced around the theme of tapping into the mind's potential via complete immersion into one and all activities. My growth became defined by *barrierlessness.* Pure concentration didn't allow thoughts or false constructions to impede my awareness, and I observed clear connections between different life experiences through the common mode of consciousness by which they were perceived.

As I cultivated openness to these connections, my life became flooded with intense learning experiences. I remember sitting on a Bermuda cliff one stormy afternoon, watching waves pound into the rocks. I was focused on the water trickling back out to sea and suddenly knew the answer to a chess problem I had been wrestling with for weeks. Another time, after completely immersing myself in the analysis of a chess position for eight hours, I had a breakthrough in my Tai Chi and successfully tested it in class that night. Great literature inspired chess growth, shooting jump shots on a New York City blacktop gave me insight about fluidity that applied to Tai Chi, becoming at peace holding my breath seventy feet underwater as a free-diver helped me in the time pressure of world championship chess or martial arts competitions. Training in the ability to quickly lower my heart rate after intense physical strain helped me recover between periods of exhausting concentration in chess tournaments. After several years of cloudiness, I was flying free, devouring information, completely in love with learning.

* * *

Before I began to conceive of this book, I was content to understand my growth in the martial arts in a very abstract manner. I related to my experience with language like *parallel learning* and *translation of level*. I felt as though I had transferred the essence of my chess understanding into my Tai Chi practice. But this didn't make much sense, especially outside of my own head. What does *essence* really mean anyway? And how does one transfer it from a mental to a physical discipline?

These questions became the central preoccupation in my life after I won my first Push Hands National Championship in November 2000. At the time I was studying philosophy at Columbia University and was especially drawn to Asian thought. I discovered some interesting foundations for my experience in ancient Indian, Chinese, Tibetan, and Greek texts—Upanishadic *essence,* Taoist *receptivity,* Neo-Confucian *principle,* Buddhist *nonduality,* and the Platonic *forms* all seemed to be a bizarre cross-cultural trace of what I was searching for. Whenever I had an idea, I would test it against some brilliant professor who usually disagreed with my conclusions. Academic minds tend to be impatient with abstract language—when I spoke about *intuition,* one philosophy professor rolled her eyes and told me the term had no meaning. The need for precision forced me to think about these ideas more concretely. I had to come to a deeper sense of concepts like *essence, quality, principle, intuition,* and *wisdom* in order to understand my own experience, let alone have any chance of communicating it.

As I struggled for a more precise grasp of my own learning process, I was forced to retrace my steps and remember what had been internalized and forgotten. In both my chess and martial arts lives, there is a method of study that has been critical to my growth. I sometimes refer to it as the study of *numbers to leave numbers,* or *form to leave form.* A basic example of this process, which applies to any discipline, can easily be illustrated through chess: A chess student must initially become immersed in the fundamentals in order to have any potential to reach a high level of skill. He or she will learn the principles of endgame, middlegame, and opening play. Initially one or two critical themes will be considered at once, but over time the intuition learns to integrate more and more principles into a sense of flow. Eventually the foundation is so deeply internalized that it is no longer consciously considered, but is lived. This process continuously cycles along as deeper layers of the art are soaked in.

Very strong chess players will rarely speak of the fundamentals, but these beacons are the building blocks of their mastery. Similarly, a great pianist or violinist does not think about individual notes, but hits them all perfectly in a virtuoso performance. In fact, thinking about a "C" while playing Beethoven's 5th Symphony could be a real hitch because the flow might be lost. The problem is that if you want to write an instructional chess book for beginners, you have to dig up all the stuff that is buried in your unconscious—I had this issue when I wrote my first book, *Attacking Chess.* In order to write for beginners, I had to break down my chess knowledge incrementally, whereas for years I had been cultivating a seamless integration of the critical information.

The same pattern can be seen when the art of learning is analyzed: themes can be internalized, lived by, and forgotten. I figured out how to learn efficiently in the brutally competitive world of chess, where a moment without growth spells a front-row seat to rivals mercilessly passing you by. Then I intuitively applied my hard-earned lessons to the martial arts. I avoided the pitfalls and tempting divergences that a learner is confronted with, but I didn't really think about them because the road map was deep inside me—just like the chess principles.

Since I decided to write this book, I have analyzed myself, taken my knowledge apart, and rigorously investigated my own experience. Speaking to corporate and academic audiences about my learning experience has also challenged me to make my ideas more accessible. Whenever there was a concept or learning technique that I related to in a manner too abstract to convey, I forced myself to break it down into the incremental steps with which I got there. Over time I began to see the principles that have been silently guiding me, and a systematic methodology of learning emerged.

My chess life began in Washington Square Park in New York's Greenwich Village, and took me on a sixteen-year-roller-coaster ride, through world championships in America, Romania, Germany, Hungary, Brazil, and India, through every kind of heartache and ecstasy a competitor can imagine. In recent years, my Tai Chi life has become a dance of meditation and intense martial competition, of pure growth and the observation, testing, and exploration of that learning process. I have currently won thirteen Tai Chi Chuan Push Hands National Championship titles, placed third in the 2002 World Championship in Taiwan, and in 2004 I won the Chung Hwa Cup International in Taiwan, the World Championship of Tai Chi Chuan Push Hands.

A lifetime of competition has not cooled my ardor to win, but I have grown to love the study and training above all else. After so many years of big games, performing under pressure has become a way of life. Presence under fire hardly feels different from the presence I feel sitting at my computer, typing these sentences. What I have realized is that what I am best at is not Tai Chi, and it is not chess—what I am best at is the art of learning. This book is the story of my method.

PART I

◆

THE FOUNDATION

CHAPTER 1

INNOCENT MOVES

I remember the cold late winter afternoon in downtown New York City, my mother and I holding hands while walking to the playground in Washington Square Park. I was six years old, a rough-and-tumble kid with a passion for Spider-Man, sharks, dinosaurs, sports, and driving my parents crazy with mischief. "Too much boy," my mom says. I constantly pestered my dad to throw around a football or baseball or to wrestle in the living room. My friends called me "waste skin" because my knees were often raw from taking spills in the playground or diving for catches. I had an early attraction to the edge, using scraps of wood and cinder blocks from a construction site next door to set up makeshift jump courses for my bike. I refused to wear a helmet until one gorgeous twist ended with a face plant and my mom vowed to no longer wear her headgear when horseback riding unless I followed suit.

We had taken this walk dozens of times. I loved to swing around on the monkey bars and become Tarzan, the world my jungle. But now something felt different. I looked over my shoulder, and was transfixed by mysterious figurines set up on a marble chessboard. I remember feeling like I was looking into a forest. The pieces were animals, filled with strange potential, as if something dangerous and magical were about to leap from the board. Two park hustlers sat across the table taunting each other. The air was thick with tension, and then the pieces exploded into action, nimble fingers moving with lightning speed and precision, white and black figures darting all over the board, creating patterns. I was pulled into the battlefield, enraptured; something felt familiar about this game, it made sense. Then a crowd gathered around the table and I couldn't see anymore. My mom called me, gently pulled on my hand, and we moved on to the playground.

A few days later my mom and I were walking through the same corner of the park when I broke away from her and ran up to an old man with a grey beard who was setting up plastic pieces on one of the marble boards. That day I had watched a couple of kids playing chess at school and I thought I could do it—"Wanna play?" The old man looked at me suspiciously over his spectacles. My mom apologized, explained that I didn't know how to play chess, but the old man said that it was okay, he had children, and he had a little time to kill. My mom tells me that when the game began my tongue was out and resting on my upper lip, a sure sign I was either stuffed up or concentrating. I remember the strange sensation of discovering a lost memory. As we moved the pieces, I felt like I had done this before. There was a harmony to this game, like a good song. The old man read a newspaper while I thought about my moves, but after a few minutes he got angry and snapped at my mom, accused her of hustling him. Apparently I was playing well.

I had generated an attack by coordinating a few of my pieces and the old man had to buckle down to fight it off.

After a little while a crowd gathered around the board—people were whispering something about "Young Fischer." My mom was confused, a little concerned about what had come over her boy. I was in my own world. Eventually the old man won the game. We shook hands and he asked me my name. He wrote it on his newspaper and said "Josh Waitzkin, I'm gonna read about you in the paper someday."

From that day forward, Washington Square Park became a second home to me. And chess became my first love. After school, instead of hungering for soccer or baseball, I insisted on heading to the park. I'd plop down against some scary-looking dude, put my game face on, and go to war. I loved the thrill of battle, and some days I would play countless speed chess games, hour after hour staring through the jungle of pieces, figuring things out, throwing mental grenades back and forth in a sweat. I would go home with chess pieces flying through my mind, and then I would ask my dad to take down his dusty wooden set and play with me.

Over time, as I became a trusted part of the park scene, the guys took me under their wings, showed me their tricks, taught me how to generate devastating attacks and get into the head of my opponent. I became a protégé of the street, hard to rattle, a feisty competitor. It was a bizarre school for a child, a rough crowd of alcoholics, homeless geniuses, wealthy gamblers hooked on the game, junkies, eccentric artists—all diamonds in the rough, brilliant, beat men, lives in shambles, aflame with a passion for chess.

Every day, unless it poured or snowed, the nineteen marble tables in the southwest corner of Washington Square would fill up with this motley crew. And most days I was there, knocking chessmen over with my short arms, chewing gum, learning the game. Of course my parents thought long and hard before allowing me to hang out in the park, but I was adamant and the guys cleaned up their acts when I came to play. The cigarettes and joints were put out, the language was cleaned up, few deals went down. I would sit across from one of my buddies, immediately sweating and focused. My mom told me she saw her little boy become an old man when I played chess. I concentrated so hard, she thought her hand would burn if she put it in front of my eyes. It is difficult for me to explain the seriousness I had about chess as a young boy. I guess it was a calling, though I'm still not sure what that means.

After a few months I could already beat a number of the guys who had been playing for decades. When I lost a game, one of my friends would give me a piece of advice—"Josh, you laid back too long, he got comfortable, you gotta go after 'em, make 'em scared" or "Josh, my man, sometimes you gotta castle, get your king to safety, check yourself before you wreck yourself." Then I would hit the clock, buckle down, and try again. Each loss was a lesson, each win a thrill. Every day pieces of the puzzle fell together.

Whenever I showed up to play, big crowds would gather around the table. I was a star in this little world, and while all the attention was exciting for a child, it was also a challenge. I learned quickly that when I thought about the people watching, I played badly. It was hard for a six-year-old ham to ignore throngs of adults talking about him, but when well focused, I seemed to hover in an in-between state where the intensity of the chess position mixed with the rumble of voices, traffic noises, ambulance sirens, all in an inspiring swirl that fueled my mind. Some days I could concentrate more purely in the chaos of Washington Square than in the quiet of my family's living room. Other days I would look around at everybody, get caught up in their conversations, and play terribly. I'm sure it was frustrating for my parents watching my early discovery of chess—there was no telling whether I'd chew gummy bears, smile, joke, and hang my pieces or buckle down into another world of intensity.

One Saturday afternoon there was a tall figure standing in the crowd while I played speed chess against my friend Jerry. I noticed him, but then fell back into the game. A couple of hours later the man approached my father and introduced himself as Bruce Pandolfini, a master-level player and a chess teacher. Bruce told my dad I was very gifted, and offered to teach me.

It turns out that my father recognized Bruce as the man who did television commentary with Shelby Lyman during the historic Bobby Fischer vs. Boris Spassky World Championship match in 1972. The match had revolutionized chess—it was a cold-war face-off pitting the Soviet World Champion along with his team of one hundred coaches and trainers against the brash renegade American challenger who did all his preparation alone in a room without a view. Fischer was a combination of James Dean and Greta Garbo and America was fascinated.

There were huge political implications to this contest of great thinkers. Increasingly, as the match unfolded, it became perceived as the embodiment of the cold war. Henry Kissinger called Bobby with support; politicians on both sides followed each game closely. The world watched breathless as Shelby and Bruce brought chess to life on television with their human, down-home analysis of the games. When Fischer won the match, he became an international celebrity and chess exploded across America. Suddenly the game

stood shoulder to shoulder with basketball, football, baseball, hockey. Then in 1975 Fischer disappeared instead of
defending his title. Chess in America receded into the shad-
ows. Ever since the American chess world has been searching
for a new Bobby Fischer, someone to bring the sport back
into the limelight.

Shelby and Bruce had captured my dad's imagination
twenty years before, and now it was a bit surreal that Bruce
was offering to teach his six-year-old bowling ball of a child.
I was nonplussed. Chess was fun, and the guys in the park
were my buddies. They were teaching me fine. Why should
I have any more coaches? I was private about chess, as if it
were an intimate fantasy world. I had to trust someone to let
them into my thought process, and Bruce had to overcome
this shield before the work could begin.

Our first lessons were anything but orthodox. We hardly
"studied chess." Bruce knew it was more important for us to
get to know one another, to establish a genuine camaraderie.
So we talked about life, sports, dinosaurs, things that interested me. Whenever the discussion turned to chess, I was
stubborn about my ideas and refused to receive formal
instruction.

I insisted on some bad habits I had learned in the park—
for example, bringing out my queen early. This is a typical
beginner's error: the queen is the most powerful piece on the
chessboard so people want to bring her into the action right
away. Against unskilled opponents who can't parry simple
attacks, this strategy works marvelously. The problem is
that since the queen cannot be traded for any of the opponent's pieces without significant loss, she can be chased all
over the board while the other guy naturally brings his less
valuable but quite potent warriors into play and simultane-

ously swats aside the primitive threats of the lone queen. Logical enough, but I resisted because I had won so many early games with a wandering queen. Bruce couldn't convince me with words—he had to prove it.

Bruce decided we should have knock-down drag-out speed chess matches like the ones I was used to in the park. Whenever I made a fundamental error, he would mention the principle I had violated. If I refused to budge, he'd proceed to take advantage of the error until my position fell apart. Over time, Bruce earned my respect as I saw the correctness of his ideas. My queen started to wait until the moment was right. I learned to develop my pieces, to control the center, to prepare attacks systematically.

Once he had won my trust, Bruce taught me by allowing me to express myself. The main obstacle to overcome was my impetuosity. I was a talented kid with good instincts who had been beating up on street hustlers who lacked classical training. Now it was time to slow me down and properly arm my intuition, but Bruce had a fine line to tread. He had to teach me to be more disciplined without dampening my love for chess or suppressing my natural voice. Many teachers have no feel for this balance and try to force their students into cookie-cutter molds. I have run into quite a few egomaniacal instructors like this over the years and have come to believe that their method is profoundly destructive for students in the long run—in any case, it certainly would not have worked with me.

I'm sure I was a tough kid to teach. My parents raised a willful child. Even as a young boy I was encouraged to take part in the spirited dinner party debates about art and politics in my family's living room. I was taught to express my opinion and to think about the ideas of others—not to follow authority blindly. Fortunately, Bruce's educational philosophy fit my character perfectly. He didn't present himself as omniscient, and he handled himself as more of a guide in my development than as an authority. If I disagreed with him, we would have a discussion, not a lecture.

Bruce slowed me down by asking questions. Whenever I made an important decision, good or bad, he would ask me to explain my thought process. Were there other ways to accomplish the same aim? Had I looked for my opponent's threats? Did I consider a different order of operations? Bruce didn't patronize me—some teachers rebel so far away from being authoritarian that they praise all their little player's decisions, good or bad. Their intention is to build confidence, but instead they discourage objectivity, encourage self-indulgence, and perhaps most destructively, they create a dishonest relationship between instructor and pupil that any bright child can sense.

When I made a bad move, Bruce asked me what my idea was and then helped me discover how I could have approached the decision-making process differently. Much of the time in our lessons was spent in silence, with us both thinking. Bruce did not want to feed me information, but to help my mind carve itself into maturity. Over time, in his coaxing, humorous, and understatedly firm manner, Bruce gave me a foundation of critical chess principles and a systematic understanding of analysis and calculation. While the new knowledge was valuable, the most important factor in these first months of study was that Bruce nurtured my love for chess, and he never let technical material smother my innate feeling for the game.

During these early months of work with Bruce, we would meet once or twice a week in my family's apartment—

sometimes early mornings, sometimes after school. Most other days, I would go to Washington Square and duke it out with my friends in the park. As a six- and seven-year-old boy I had two powerful currents to my chess education, and the key was to make them coexist peacefully—the street-tough competitor had to fuse with the classically trained, patient player that Bruce was inspiring. Though when very young I was periodically reluctant about real chess work, I loved the sublime beauty of old World Championship games I studied with Bruce—sometimes sitting in silence and calculating an endgame position for twenty minutes would thrill me to the core. But other times such serious thinking would bore me and I'd hunger to play speed chess with my buddies, to attack, to be a little reckless and create beautiful combinations. The park was fun. I was a child after all.

Despite significant outside pressure, my parents and Bruce decided to keep me out of tournaments until I had been playing chess for a year or so, because they wanted my relationship to the game to be about learning and passion first, and competition a distant second. My mother and Bruce were particularly ambivalent about exposing me to the harsh pressures of competitive chess—they gave me some extra months of innocence for which I am grateful. When I finally started playing in scholastic tournaments, soon after my seventh birthday, the games felt easy. Children my own age didn't fashion complicated attacks and defenses like the guys in the park did, and they would crumble under pressure. Some of the kids were armed with dangerous opening traps, memorized variations that could lead to early advantages, so I often came out of the opening down a pawn or two—but then they didn't have a chance. For me, competitive chess was not about perfection. It was more of a mental prizefight, with two opponents trading advantages, momentum going one way and then the other. My friends in Washington Square were valiant competitors, you could never count them out—in fact they were most dangerous when on the ropes. Many very talented kids expected to win without much resistance. When the game was a struggle, they were emotionally unprepared.

I thrived under adversity. My style was to make the game complex and then work my way through the chaos. When the position was wild, I had huge confidence. Bruce and I also spent a lot of time studying endgames, where the board is nearly empty and high-level principles combine with deep calculations to create fascinating battles. While my opponents wanted to win in the openings, right off the bat, I guided positions into complicated middlegames and abstract endings. So as the game went on, their confidence shrank and I became a predator. Noticing these tendencies, Bruce started calling me "Tiger." He still calls me Tiger today.

My first year of competitive chess was smooth sailing. I felt unbeatable when matched up with kids my age, and the combination of street toughness and classical education proved devastating for my opponents. Perhaps the most decisive element of my game was the way my style on the board was completely in synch with my personality as a child. I was unhindered by internal conflict—a state of being that I have come to see as fundamental to the learning process. Bruce and the park guys had taught me how to express myself through chess, and so my love for the game grew every day.

As the months went by, I piled up win after win and my national rating skyrocketed. I'd show up at a tournament and kids were terrified of me, which felt strange. I was, after all, a young child who was scared of the dark and loved Scooby-Doo. More than once, opponents started weeping at the board before the game had even begun. I felt bad for them but also empowered. Before I knew it I was the highest-ranked player for my age in the country. The next step was the National Championship, to be held in Charlotte, North Carolina. The guys in the park were buzzing with excitement, showing me more and more weapons, honing my game. I was the hands-down favorite to win the primary division (kindergarten through 3rd grade). There wasn't a doubt in my mind.

CHAPTER 2

Losing to Win

Primary School National Chess Championship
Charlotte, North Carolina
May 5, 1985.

Last round. Board one. Winner takes the title. My opponent and I were set up on a solitary table in front of an unmanned camera that would relay the position to press, coaches, and anxiety-ridden parents in the hotel lobby. The rest of the competitors, over five hundred of the country's top young chess players who had come to battle for the National Championships, faced off on long rows of chessboards filling up the rest of the tense playing hall. The top board is a throne or a prison, depending on how you look at it. Everyone dreams of getting there, but then you arrive and find yourself all alone, trapped on a pedestal with a bull's-eye on your forehead. Entering the tournament, I was the man to beat. I knew teams had been gunning for me, spending months of preparation on treacherous opening traps designed specifically to catch me off guard. But I had already rolled over my first six opponents, giving up only one draw. I felt unbeatable when matched up against kids my age. They couldn't touch me.

Little did I know that my opponent was a well-armed genius. His name was David Arnett. At three years old he had memorized the New York City subway map. At five he was doing high school math. At six he was the top first-grader in the country and the best chess player at the prestigious Dalton School, which was coached by Svetozar Jovanovic, a legend in scholastic chess who had taught many young champions. Jovanovic had given David a classical chess education and a sense for competitive discipline to rival my own. Soon after this game, Dave and I would become best friends. But right now he was just a buck-toothed little blond kid who looked petrified.

On the third move of the game, David made a strange decision, allowing me to capture his king pawn with my knight. I should have taken some time to look for traps, but I moved too quickly. Then he was all over me, bringing his queen into a dangerous attacking position, chasing my overextended knight who had nowhere safe to hide. I'd been stupid to grab the pawn. Now this smart little kid was going after my king and I was fighting for my life.

I can see my eight-year-old self as the game slipped away, sitting at the board, sweat beginning to flow, goose bumps rising, my heart picking up speed, hungry stares of envious rivals sitting at nearby chessboards, the eerie rustling silence of the playing hall, the fragility of so many dreams. I wasn't a superman. I was a child who slept in my parents' bedroom because of terrible nightmares, now competing with the world on my shoulders and everything falling apart.

I had a choice of completely self-destructing or losing some material, regrouping, and then trying to fight back.

I'd done this countless times at Washington Square Park. But being on the ropes against a kid was new to me. I had dealt with the pressures of being the favorite at the Nationals by puffing myself up with a sense of invincibility. Confidence is critical for a great competitor, but overconfidence is brittle. We are too smart for ourselves in such moments. We sense our mortality like a cancer beneath the bravado, and when things start to go out of control, there is little real resilience to fall back on.

When the game was over I was stunned, reeling from being so close to winning my first national championship and then letting it go, self-destructing, falling apart. Was I a loser? Had I let my parents down? What about the guys in the park, Bruce, my friends at school? How could I have lost? One of the problems with being too high is that there is a long way to fall. Had I fallen in my own eyes or also in the eyes of those around me? After trying so hard, was there worth outside of winning? An eight-year-old is hardly prepared to deal with such loaded issues, and I was very fortunate to have a family with the ability to keep, or at least regain, a bit of perspective in times of extreme intensity. We went fishing.

*   *   *

The ocean has been a huge part of my life since the womb. Literally. When my mother was five months pregnant, we were at sea, trolling for blue marlin in ten-foot Gulf Stream rollers. Some of my earliest memories are from the dock of my family's little house on mosquito-ridden South Bimini Island, fishing for snappers, feeding moray eels, swatting away bugs at night while chumming for sharks.

Growing up, I knew that come summertime, we would

head off to sea no matter what else was happening in our lives, what crisis was looming, what tournaments I was missing, how out of context or absurd our ocean trips might have felt at the moment of departure. I have come to understand that these little breaks from the competitive intensity of my life have been and still are an integral part of my success. Times at sea are periods of renewal, coming together with family, being with nature, putting things back in perspective. I am able to let my conscious mind move away from my training, and to gain creative new angles on the next steps of my growth. These trips are a far cry from luxurious vacations—actually they are nonstop manual labor, sweating in the engine room trying to coax an old generator back to life, working the cockpit in the hot sun, keeping the boat together in angry squalls, navigating through big seas, living right on the edge.

The boating life has also been a wonderful training ground for performance psychology. Living on the water requires constant presence, and the release of control. A boat is always moving with the sea, lurching beneath your feet, and the only way to survive is to sink into rhythm with the waves and be ready for anything. I learned at sea that virtually all situations can be handled as long as presence of mind is maintained. On the other hand, if you lose your calm when crisis hits seventy miles from land, or while swimming with big sharks, there is no safety net to catch you.

There have been many years when leaving my New York life felt like career suicide—my chess rivals were taking lessons and competing in every weekend tournament while I was on a boat crashing through big waves. But I would come back with new ideas and a full tank of energy and determination. The ocean has always healed me, brought me back to life when I have needed it . . . and as an eight-year-old child in the midst of an existential crisis, I needed it.

My parents, baby sister, and I left Fort Lauderdale on the *Ebb Tide,* our twenty-four-foot Black Fin, a wonderful old fishing boat that carried us through many summer adventures in high seas until she blew up and sank when I was twelve. Fifty-seven miles east southeast was Bimini, an island that was like home to me. I can still see her coming into sight through my childhood eyes, those hazy first trees like a miracle after a long ocean crossing. We didn't talk about chess for weeks. We fished, dove in warm crystal-clear water, trolled the Gulf Stream, breathed in the beautiful southern air. I rediscovered myself as a child, ran around the island with my friends Kier and Kino, passed countless hours with my head hanging off our rickety old dock, hand line dangling in the water, watching the fish dart around. On rainy evenings, my mom and I would take our dog Brownie and go into the jungle, hunting for giant land crab. My family reconnected as human beings, outside of the mad swirl of scholastic chess. I was devastated, but slowly my parents revived my boyish enthusiasm for life.

In painful times, my mom has always been an anchor, holding everything together until the clouds roll by. When I was a child, she would press her soft cheek against mine, reminding me that I didn't always have to be so tough. I didn't have to tell her how I felt—she knew. My mother is the greatest person I have ever known. She is a brilliant, loving, compassionate woman with a wisdom that to this day blows my mind. Quietly powerful, infinitely supportive, absurdly selfless, she has always encouraged me to follow my heart even when it led far away or to seemingly bizarre pursuits. She is also incredibly brave (sometimes to my dismay), facing down four-hundred-pound sharks in deep ocean, hand-lining leaping blue marlin, taming wild two-thousand-pound stallions, breaking up street fights, keeping my dad and me in line. She has been a constant balancing force throughout all the madness of our lives—lifting us when we were down, providing perspective when we got too swept away by ambition, giving a hug when tears flowed. My mom is my hero. Without her the whole thing falls apart.

My father is a different type of character. He's a loyal, emotional, eccentric (think Woody Allen meets Larry David with an adventurous spin), devoted dad who has been my best friend since day one. I can't imagine how many hours we have spent together, playing basketball, throwing around footballs and baseballs, scouring ocean horizons for birds above schooling fish, traveling to chess tournaments and then martial arts championships all over the world. We have been an elite team since I was six years old and subsequently have been joined at the hip in our ambitions and, to a certain extent, our emotions. No matter how much perspective we tried to maintain, our senses of well-being often fluctuated with my competitive results. There was no way around this. After winning huge tournaments, all was well and the sky was the limit. When I was playing badly, everything could look bleak and our dreams absurd.

It is true that I played with the knowledge that my dad's heart was on the line side by side with my own—but I also knew that he would love me regardless of the outcome. There is little question that some psychologists would frown upon such co-dependence between father and son, but when you are pursuing the pinnacle sometimes limits must be pushed. There are big games, climactic moments, final surges where you dig for energy and inspiration wherever you can find it and pick up the pieces later. One thing is for sure—through thick and thin, my dad has always been in my corner 100 percent.

After a month on Bimini, my pop got restless and arranged a match between me and the best chess player on the island. He was worried that I was taking too long away from the game, and also he was just itching to see me play again. I wasn't so eager for the match, preferring to fish with my hand line and go diving for lobster. Chess was still a burden to me, but the idea of the Championship of Bimini sounded harmless and amusing. We tracked down the guy and faced off in a bar. He had gold teeth, and a huge gold necklace hanging down over the board—remnants of a drug-smuggling past. It took me a few minutes to get into the games but then I came alive, the old love trickling back. I recall the feeling of inevitability, like chess was part of me, not to be denied. Something steeled in my eight-year-old self that summer—I wouldn't go out a loser.

When I got home in the fall, Bruce was preoccupied with book deadlines and had no time for me. He cancelled lesson after lesson, which felt like a terrible slap in the face. I had lost and now my teacher didn't like me. The equation was simple. When we did meet, his mind was elsewhere and the lessons were technical and alienating. Maybe he was busy, but I was a kid in need.

I also transferred from the Little Red School House to the prestigious Dalton School on the upper east side of Manhattan. The transition was difficult—instead of a few blocks from home, school was now a long bus ride away. I missed my friends at Little Red and felt out of place with all the rich kids at Dalton. I remember the first time a couple of us went over to my new friend's apartment uptown and I walked into what seemed like a palace. There were doormen and maids and chandeliers hanging from duplexed ceilings. I was confused by all this stuff and began to wonder if my family was somehow inferior. I am still ashamed of the memory of asking my dad to park around the corner when he came to pick me up so my friends wouldn't see our beat-up green Plymouth that had a shot suspension and an alarming habit of jumping lanes on the West Side Drive.

I was a mess. My chess life had fallen apart, my teacher didn't like me anymore, I missed my friends, and my family didn't have a doorman or a fancy car. On top of all this a pretty girl I had a crush on at school had developed the habit of hitting me over the head with her shoes, which I didn't realize (until she told me many years later) was a sign that she shared my feelings. I was a child in transition, and I needed some help getting through. A few weeks into the fall, Bruce saw that rushing through mechanical chess analysis was not what I needed, and so he took a step back and reconceived our chess life. Our lessons now included raucous speed chess sessions with breaks to toss a football outside. We began to laugh and connect as human beings as we had in our first sessions years before.

I went back to playing in Washington Square Park with my old buddies. The game became less haunted. I was having fun again. Then Bruce and I went to work. We plunged deep into the heart of the art, analyzing complex middlegame and endgame positions, studying the classics, developing my technical understanding. We started doing arduous visualization work, playing blindfold chess games and working through long variations in our heads, without moving the pieces.

Chess was different now. During those summer months

when I questioned everything and decided to come back strong, I arrived at a commitment to chess that was about much more than fun and glory. It was about love and pain and passion and pushing myself to overcome. It might sound absurd, but I believe that year, from eight to nine, was the defining period of my life. I responded to heartbreak with hard work. I was self-motivated and moved by a powerful resolve. While a young boy, I had been all promise. I only knew winning because I was better than all the other children and there was no pressure competing against adults. Now there was the knowledge of my mortality. I had lost to a kid, and there were other children who were also dangerous rivals.

I was still the highest-rated player for my age in the country, and when I went to tournaments there was immense pressure. If I won, it was no big deal, but if I lost it felt like the sky would fall. There was one boy who was particularly alarming. His name was Jeff Sarwer. He was a scary child—small, often bald and barefoot. He didn't go to school and his father had him studying chess twelve hours a day. When he played, Jeff would chant *kill, kill, kill* under his breath. The kid was all aggression, brilliant, a powerhouse over the board. When I had just gotten back from my summer away I arrived at the Manhattan Chess Club for a lesson with Bruce, and Jeff was sitting there playing a regular. He approached me with a challenge, which I accepted. I was rusty and not expecting much of a game—he blew me away. A couple of months later I went back to the Manhattan and returned the favor with a huge crowd surrounding the board. After I beat him, I heard that he sat crying in a corner for hours. Terrible. This was a bitter rivalry between children, and it felt like the end of the earth.

I spent many afternoons studying chess in my room, alone. Sometimes my dad tried to distract me, lure me away to play football or basketball, and I would have none of it. There was too much on the line. My parents worried that I had become too serious about chess, and my dad periodically told me that it was okay if I wanted to quit. They didn't understand that quitting was not an option.

As the Nationals approached, my training got even more intense. I sharpened myself in the park, soaked in the street-smart advice of my hustler friends, and did more and more serious work with Bruce. I knew Sarwer was spending every waking minute working with Grandmasters, honing his razor-sharp game. He was a machine, annihilating strong adults in speed chess sessions and then humiliating them with his disdain. One day he showed up at the park when I wasn't there, and all my buddies told him I was better. He laughed, and said "Josh is a putz." They taunted him until he left my home turf. The New York chess scene was divided between his camp and mine. This was not child's play anymore.

The Nationals were again held in Charlotte, North Carolina. I traveled to the tournament with my parents, baby sister Katya, and Bruce. This was the first tournament to which Bruce had ever come with me. He was not a competitor at heart and was deeply conflicted about children tearing each other apart under such pressure. I don't really blame him. Three close friends of mine from Little Red also came to hang out at the tournament with their parents. They weren't really chess players—this was more of a vacation for them. I was deadly serious. I played my games on the first board, isolated from the rest of the children once more. My parents waited in the hotel lobby, watching my game on a video monitor with throngs of other nervous moms and dads. My first round was difficult, but then I cruised through the field, winning my first six games.

Going into the last round, Jeff Sarwer and I had the only two perfect scores. I had harder pairings throughout the event, so if we drew the game I would win on tie-breaks—but no one was thinking draw.

Jeff was the only kid I was afraid of. Rumor was that he, his father, and sister had been sleeping in their car throughout the tournament. Between rounds he would sit on the floor, hugging his skinny knees and scowling at anyone who tried to speak to him. He had contempt for other kids, called them "ugly putzes" and smirked when approached. It would be easy to vilify him, but Jeff was a child dealt certain cards. His father was a brutal authoritarian, a messianic figure who channeled his crazy energy and ideas into creating the perfect chess machine. Although we never really connected on a personal level, I had great respect for Jeff. He loved the game and worked at it harder than anyone I knew. This would be war.

He had the white pieces, a small advantage (white moves first) that was magnified by our particular matchup. I had done a lot of preparation on the white side of my opening repertoire and was less confident with black. He started the game with tremendous aggression, coming straight after me with a very dangerous central pawn storm against my King's Indian Defense. I had never seen this variation before. He moved quickly, playing with terrifying confidence, and I was on the ropes from the start. His central pawn phalanx seemed to be devouring me, pushing me back before the game even began. He bristled with cockiness and seemed to mock me, implying that I had no right to sit at his chessboard.

My chances looked slim right off the bat. Early in the middlegame I lost a pawn and then I tried to slow down his initiative by trading some pieces. This is risky—when you are down material, exchanging pieces increases your opponent's advantage (consider how the ratio of 5 to 4 compares to 4 to 3; 3 to 2; 2 to 1; 1 to 0—as pieces come off the chessboard, a small material edge can gradually become overwhelming). But I loved the endgame, and headed for it like a safe house. When we traded queens Jeff seemed to snarl at me. He was an absolute killer, and he had me by the throat.

After three hours, the tournament hall was empty as we reached the end of the game. We were alone but for the television camera that was broadcasting to the hotel lobby where hundreds of people were gathered around the monitor, watching and wondering which little kid would be the champ and which would be crushed. The silence was suffocating—or maybe that was just my position. I had a knight and five pawns against his bishop and six pawns. It looked hopeless. I remember wrestling with the demons of the previous year's heartbreaker while I searched for a way out. Nothing there. I went to the bathroom and cried. Then I washed my face, steeled myself, buckled down and went back to the board.

It was as if I was trapped in dark jungle, stuck in the underbrush, starving, bleeding and suddenly there was a little light. I'll never forget the feeling when I sensed my potential escape. Often in chess, you feel something is there before you find it. The skin suddenly perks up, senses heighten like an animal feeling danger or prey. The unconscious alerts the conscious player that there is something to be found, and then the search begins. I started calculating, putting things together. Slowly the plan crystallized in my mind. I had to take my knight out of play and give up my remaining pawns to set up a long combination that would leave just two kings on the board—a completely counter-intuitive idea. I found moves that were far beyond my years to save that game and I'm not really sure how I did it.

We drew the game and I became National Champion. I walked out of the playing hall in a daze, and was hit by a mob of cheering kids and parents who had been sucked into the drama of the battle. One coach, an International Master, asked me why I had made a certain decision in the middlegame and I had no idea what he was talking about. Chess was already a world away. The humanity of the moment was overwhelming. I watched Jeff slip around the crowd and approach his father, who rejected him with a cold stare. It was awful.

CHAPTER 3

Two Approaches
to Learning

As you can probably sense, the scholastic chess world is a deadly place. Every year, thousands of boys and girls put their hearts on the line, each child believing he or she may be the best. Glory is a powerful incentive. Inevitably dreams are dashed, hearts are broken, most fall short of their expectations because there is little room at the top. Of course this dynamic can be found in virtually any ambitious field. Little League athletes dream of playing for their favorite Major League team. Kids shooting hoops in the schoolyards want to be like Mike. The world of actors and musicians is brimming with huge expectations, wild competitiveness, and a tiny window of realistic possibility.

Two questions arise. First, what is the difference that allows some to fit into that narrow window to the top? And second, what is the point? If ambition spells probable disappointment, why pursue excellence? In my opinion, the answer to both questions lies in a well-thought-out approach that inspires resilience, the ability to make connections between diverse pursuits, and day-to-day enjoyment of the

29

process. The vast majority of motivated people, young and old, make terrible mistakes in their approach to learning. They fall frustrated by the wayside while those on the road to success keep steady on their paths.

Developmental psychologists have done extensive research on the effects of a student's approach on his or her ability to learn and ultimately master material. Dr. Carol Dweck, a leading researcher in the field of developmental psychology, makes the distinction between *entity* and *incremental* theories of intelligence. Children who are "entity theorists"—that is, kids who have been influenced by their parents and teachers to think in this manner—are prone to use language like "I am smart at this" and to attribute their success or failure to an ingrained and unalterable level of ability. They see their overall intelligence or skill level at a certain discipline to be a fixed *entity,* a thing that cannot evolve. Incremental theorists, who have picked up a different modality of learning—let's call them *learning theorists*—are more prone to describe their results with sentences like "I got it because I worked very hard at it" or "I should have tried harder." A child with a learning theory of intelligence tends to sense that with hard work, difficult material can be grasped—step by step, *incrementally,* the novice can become the master.

Dweck's research has shown that when challenged by difficult material, learning theorists are far more likely to rise to the level of the game, while entity theorists are more brittle and prone to quit. Children who associate success with hard work tend to have a "mastery-oriented response" to challenging situations, while children who see themselves as just plain "smart" or "dumb," or "good" or "bad" at something, have a "learned helplessness orientation."

In one wonderfully revealing study, a group of children was interviewed and then each child was noted as having either an entity or learning theory of intelligence. All the children were then given a series of easy math problems, which they all solved correctly. Then, all the children were given some very hard problems to solve—problems that were too difficult for them. It was clear that the learning theorists were excited by the challenge, while the entity theorists were dismayed. Comments would range from "Oh boy, now I'm really gonna have to try hard" to "I'm not smart enough for this." Everyone got these problems wrong— but evidently the experience of being challenged had very different effects. What is most interesting is the third stage of this experiment: all the children were once again given easy problems to solve. Nearly all of the learning theorists breezed right through the easy material, but the entity theorists had been so dispirited by the inability to solve the hard problems that many of them foundered through the easy stuff. Their self-confidence had been destroyed.

What is compelling about this is that the results have nothing to do with intelligence level. Very smart kids with entity theories tend to be far more brittle when challenged than kids with learning theories who would be considered not quite as sharp. In fact, some of the brightest kids prove to be the most vulnerable to becoming helpless, because they feel the need to live up to and maintain a perfectionist image that is easily and inevitably shattered. As an observer of countless talented young chess players, I can vouch for the accuracy of this point—some of the most gifted players are the worst under pressure, and have the hardest time rebounding from defeat.

How are these theories of intelligence programmed into

our minds? Often subtle differences in parental or instructional style can make a huge difference. Entity theorists tend to have been told that they did well when they have succeeded, and that they weren't any good at something when they have failed. So a kid aces a math test, comes home, and hears "Wow, that's my boy! As smart as they come!" Then, next week Johnny fails an English test and hears "What's wrong with you? Can't you read?" or "Your Mommy never liked reading either—obviously, it's not your thing." So the boy figures he's good at math and bad at English, and what's more, he links success and failure to ingrained ability. Learning theorists, on the other hand, are given feedback that is more process-oriented. After doing well on an English essay, a little girl might be congratulated by her teacher with "Wow, great job Julie! You're really becoming a wonderful writer! Keep up the good work!" And if she does badly on a math test, her teacher might write "Study a little harder for the next one and you'll do great! And feel free to ask me questions any time after class, that's what I'm here for!" So Julie learns to associate effort with success and feels that she can become good at anything with some hard work. She also feels as though she is on a journey of learning, and her teacher is a friendly assistant in her growth. Johnny thinks he's good at math and bad at English, and he focuses on quick results as opposed to long-term process—but what happens when he does badly on a hard math test down the line? Will he be prepared to learn the right lessons from life's inevitable challenges? Unfortunately, he may not.

It is clear that parents and teachers have an enormous responsibility in forming the theories of intelligence of their students and children—and it is never too late. It is critical to realize that we can always evolve in our approaches to learning. Studies have shown that in just minutes, kids can be conditioned into having a healthy learning theory for a given situation. In one study, children were given different instructions about what the aim of their task was. Some kids were told that solving certain problems would help them with their schoolwork in the future, and other kids were told that they would be judged based on their results. In other words, half the kids received "mastery-oriented" instructions, and half the kids received "helplessness-producing" instructions. Needless to say, the kids who were temporarily mastery-oriented did much better on the tests.

So how does all this affect us in our day-to-day lives? Fundamentally. The key to pursuing excellence is to embrace an organic, long-term learning process, and not to live in a shell of static, safe mediocrity. Usually, growth comes at the expense of previous comfort or safety. The hermit crab is a colorful example of a creature that lives by this aspect of the growth process (albeit without our psychological baggage). As the crab gets bigger, it needs to find a more spacious shell. So the slow, lumbering creature goes on a quest for a new home. If an appropriate new shell is not found quickly, a terribly delicate moment of truth arises. A soft creature that is used to the protection of built-in armor must now go out into the world, exposed to predators in all its mushy vulnerability. That learning phase in between shells is where our growth can spring from. Someone stuck with an entity theory of intelligence is like an anorexic hermit crab, starving itself so it doesn't grow to have to find a new shell.

In my experience, successful people shoot for the stars, put their hearts on the line in every battle, and ultimately discover that the lessons learned from the pursuit of excellence mean much more than the immediate trophies and glory. In the long run, painful losses may prove much more valuable than wins—those who are armed with a healthy attitude and are able to draw wisdom from every experience, "good" or "bad," are the ones who make it down the road. They are also the ones who are happier along the way. Of course the real challenge is to stay in range of this long-term perspective when you are under fire and hurting in the middle of the war. This, maybe our biggest hurdle, is at the core of the art of learning.

*   *   *

Let's return to the scholastic chess world, and focus on the ingredients to my early success. I mentioned that Bruce and I studied the endgame while other young players focused on the opening. In light of the entity/incremental discussion, I'd like to plunge a little more deeply into the approach that Bruce and I adopted.

Rewind to those days when I was a six-year-old prankster. Once he had won my confidence, Bruce began our study with a barren chessboard. We took on positions of reduced complexity and clear principles. Our first focus was king and pawn against king—just three pieces on the table. Over time, I gained an excellent intuitive feel for the power of the king and the subtlety of the pawn. I learned the principle of opposition, the hidden potency of empty space, the idea of *zugzwang* (putting your opponent in a position where any move he makes will destroy his position). Layer by layer we built up my knowledge and my *understanding of how to transform axioms into fuel for creative insight.* Then we turned to rook endings, bishop endings, knight endings, spending hundreds of hours as I turned seven and eight years old, exploring the operating principles behind positions that I might never see again. This method of study gave me a feeling for the beautiful subtleties of each chess piece, because in relatively clear-cut positions I could focus on what was essential. I was also gradually internalizing a marvelous methodology of learning—the play between knowledge, intuition, and creativity. From both educational and technical perspectives, I learned from the foundation up.

Most of my rivals, on the other hand, began by studying opening variations. There is a vast body of theory that begins from the starting position of all chess games, and it is very tempting to teach children openings right off the bat, because built into this theoretical part of the game there are many imbedded traps, land mines that allow a player to win quickly and easily—in effect, to win without having to struggle to win. At first thought, it seems logical for a novice to study positions that he or she will see all the time at the outset of games. Why not begin from the beginning, especially if it leads to instant success? The answer is quicksand. Once you start with openings, there is no way out. Lifetimes can be spent memorizing and keeping up with the evolving Encyclopedia of Chess Openings (ECO). They are an addiction, with perilous psychological effects.

It is a little like developing the habit of stealing the test from your teacher's desk instead of learning how to do the math. You may pass the test, but you learn absolutely nothing—and most critically, you don't gain an appreciation for the value or beauty of learning itself. For children who focus early on openings, chess becomes about results. Period. It doesn't matter how you played or if you concentrated well or if you were brave. These kids talk about the 4 move mate and ask each other, "How many moves did it take you to win"? Chess becomes one-dimensional—winning and winning fast.

Children who begin their chess education by memorizing openings tend to internalize an entity theory of intelligence. Their dialogues with teachers, parents, and other children are all about results, not effort. They consider themselves winners because so far they have won. In school, they focus on what comes easy to them and ignore the subjects that are harder. On the playground, they use the famous "I wasn't trying" after missing a shot or striking out.

Once I was in Arizona giving a lecture and simultaneous exhibition* to a large group of young chess players and parents, and the organizer of the event picked me up at the airport bragging that his son hadn't lost a chess game in over a year. Obviously this was a record the whole family was proud of. I knew what was coming—classic anorexic hermit crab. When I met the child, he was a moderately talented boy who was the best in his school. He had learned some quick opening attacks and had a natural feel for basic chess tactics. Clearly he had started winning and had been praised effusively for his genius. As a result, the boy refused to play anyone outside of the circle of friends and competitors whom he knew to be inferior (his favorite opponent was his father, who was a weak player and no challenge at all). To his

---

*A simultaneous exhibition, also referred to as a "simul," is an event where one stronger chess player competes against a large number of opponents. When I give simuls, usually there is a preceding competition to determine who will play me. Then 20–50 boards are set up in a large square of a banquet hall, and I walk from table to table inside the square while my opponents sit at their board and play one chess game. When I arrive at a board, the other makes his or her move. I then respond and move onto the next board. Simuls are an excellent way to demonstrate the understanding and visualization skills of a strong player.

school buddies, this boy was a chess god, but compared to serious chess-playing children around the country, he had a long way to go. He was a big fish in a small pond and he liked it that way. The boy avoided chess throughout my visit. He didn't want to play in the simultaneous exhibition and was the only child at the event who was resistant to instruction. His winning streak and the constant talk of it had him all locked up—he was terrified of shattering the façade of perfection. This child was paralyzed by an ever-deepening cycle of entity indoctrination.

Many kids like this are quite talented, so they excel at first because of good genes—but then they hit a roadblock. As chess struggles become more intense and opponents put up serious resistance, they start to lose interest in the game. They try to avoid challenges, but eventually the real world finds them. Their confidence is fragile. Losing is always a crisis instead of an opportunity for growth—if they were a winner because they won, this new losing must make them a loser.

The long-term effects of "opening madness" are clear, but there are also serious immediate weaknesses in young chess players brought up in this environment. Just as there are inevitable ups and downs in a career, there are also momentum shifts in individual games. Most of my early rivals were gifted children, and they were prepared with hundreds of traps with which they could win right off the bat. Playing against these kids was like walking through a minefield, but I was good enough on my feet to navigate most of the danger. I often came out of the openings in a little bit of trouble, but then I took control. As our games progressed, my opponents moved away from their area of comfort while I grew stronger and more confident. They wanted to win before the battle began, but I loved the struggle that was the heart of chess. In both the short term and the long term, these kids were crippled by the horizon imposed on them by their teachers.

The problem in the chess world is that many coaches work in schools with an ever-replenishing annual supply of talented young children. These kids are like raw material in a factory. Each year, the teachers are expected to provide results because having a nationally ranked chess team is prestigious for the school. So the coaches create a legion of entity-theorizing, tactically gifted young chess players who are armed to the teeth with a brutal opening repertoire. It doesn't matter if these kids will hit a crisis in seventh grade, because all that counts for the coach are the primary and elementary school divisions and there are always more first-graders coming up the pipe. Clearly, parents bear an enormous responsibility in navigating these issues and choosing the right teacher for their child.

I have used chess to illustrate this entity/incremental dynamic, but the issue is fundamental to the pursuit of excellence in all fields. If a young basketball player is taught that winning is the only thing that winners do, then he will crumble when he misses his first big shot. If a gymnast or ballet dancer is taught that her self-worth is entirely wrapped up in a perfectly skinny body that is always ready for performance, then how can she handle injuries or life after an inevitably short career? If a businessperson cultivates a perfectionist self-image, then how can she learn from her mistakes?

When I reflect back on my chess career, I remember the losses, and the lessons learned from defeat. I remember losing that first National Championship to David Arnett. I remember being crushed by my archrival in a sudden-death playoff of the U.S. Junior (Under 21) Championship a year before I won the tournament outright. Then there was the final round of the Under 18 World Chess Championship in Szeged, Hungary. I was on board one competing against the Russian for the world title—inches from a life's dream, I was offered a draw, a chance to share the glory. All I had to do was shake hands, but I declined, pushed for a win, and lost—such agony! These moments in my life were wracked with pain, but they were also defining gut-checks packed with potential. The setbacks taught me how to succeed. And what kept me on my path was a love for learning that has its roots in my first chess lessons as a six-year-old boy.

CHAPTER 4

LOVING THE GAME

After I won my first National Championship, my chess life started gathering momentum. My passion for the game fueled a long ride of unhindered learning and inspired performance. From nine to seventeen, I was the top-ranked player for my age in the country. I won eight individual National Championship titles, captained my school to winning seven team Nationals, and represented America in six World Championships. These were years of tremendous growth, and as I got deeper into the heart of chess, the art became a riveting window of self-exploration.

A key ingredient to my success in those years was that my style on the chessboard was a direct expression of my personality. It is my nature to revel in apparent chaos. I've always loved thunderstorms, blizzards, hurricanes, rough seas, sharky waters. Since childhood, inclement conditions have inspired me, and as a young competitor I would guide critical chess games into positions of tremendous complexity with the confidence that I would be able to sort through the mayhem more effectively than my opponents. I often sensed a logical thread to positions that seemed irrational—playing exciting chess felt like discovering hidden harmonies. I was a free-flowing performer, unblocked by psychological issues and hungering for creative leaps.

One of the most critical strengths of a superior competitor in any discipline—whether we are speaking about sports, business negotiations, or even presidential debates—is the ability to dictate the tone of the battle. Many of my young chess rivals preferred to keep the game in control. They played openings that they had memorized, played them over and over again. They hankered for rating points, calculated what the next result would do to their national ranking, and their materialistic dispositions made them uncomfortable in the stormy positions in which I thrived. Because of my classical chess education and my love for the endgame as well as crazy middlegames, I was usually able to move the position toward one of my strengths.

Things got a bit more complicated when I was ten years old and I started to compete almost exclusively in adult tournaments, only playing kids in the Nationals or World Championships. This was a big change because highly experienced tournament players could often guide the chess position into closed, strategical battles which were not to my liking. As I cultivated my strengths, I also had to take on the more abstract elements of high-level chess so I could compete effectively with more seasoned opponents. Just as muscles get stronger when they are pushed, good competitors tend to rise to the level of the opposition. The adult chess world toughened me up, made me introspective and always on the lookout for flaws to be improved on. A bonus to playing grown-ups is that whenever I competed in a scholastic Nationals I had tremendous confidence—these were only kids after all.

The transition to open tournaments also forced me to

take on the issue of endurance. In scholastic events, a single chess game rarely lasts more than three hours. In most adult competitions, each player has to make his or her first forty moves in two hours (a four-hour time control). Then there is an additional hour for each player for every succeeding twenty moves. If enough moves are played, a game can continue for what feels to a child like eternity. Older opponents know that kids have less stamina for long battles, so they sometimes made the games drag on to tire me out. Once in Philadelphia, a ruthless fellow made me play for over nine hours. I was ten years old and he sat stalling at the board in front of obvious moves for forty-five minutes at a time. It was terrible, but a lesson learned. On top of everything else, I had to develop the ability to run a mental marathon.

Chess was a constant challenge. My whole career, my father and I searched out opponents who were a little stronger than me, so even as I dominated the scholastic circuit, losing was part of my regular experience. I believe this was important for maintaining a healthy perspective on the game. While there was a lot of pressure on my shoulders, fear of failure didn't move me so much as an intense passion for the game. I think the arc of losing a heartbreaker before winning my first big title gave me license to compete on the edge.

This is not to say that losing didn't hurt. It did. There is something particularly painful about being beaten in a chess game. In the course of a battle, each player puts every ounce of his or her tactical, strategical, emotional, physical, and spiritual being into the struggle. The brain is pushed through terrible trials; we stretch every fiber of our mental capacity; the whole body aches from exhaustion after hours of rapt concentration. In the course of a dynamic chess fight, there will be shifts in momentum, near misses, narrow escapes, innovative creations, and precise refutations. When your position teeters on the brink of disaster, it feels like your life is on the line. When you win, you survive another day. When you lose, it is as if someone has torn out your heart and stepped on it. No exaggeration. Losing is brutal.

This brings up an incipient danger in what may appear to be an incremental approach. I have seen many people in diverse fields take some version of the process-first philosophy and transform it into an excuse for never putting themselves on the line or pretending not to care about results. They claim to be egoless, to care only about learning, but really this is an excuse to avoid confronting themselves. This issue of process vs. goal is very delicate, and I want to carefully define how I feel the question should be navigated.

It would be easy to read about the studies on entity vs. incremental theories of intelligence and come to the conclusion that a child should never win or lose. I don't believe this is the case. If that child discovers any ambition to pursue excellence in a given field later in life, he or she may lack the toughness to handle inevitable obstacles. While a fixation on results is certainly unhealthy, short-term goals can be useful developmental tools if they are balanced within a nurturing long-term philosophy. Too much sheltering from results can be stunting. The road to success is not easy or else everyone would be the greatest at what they do—we need to be psychologically prepared to face the unavoidable challenges along our way, and when it comes down to it, the only way to learn how to swim is by getting in the water.

Let's put ourselves in the shoes of the mother of a talented young chess player I know named Danny. This seven-year-old boy just loves chess. He can't get enough. He studies chess for a half hour every day, plays on the Internet, and takes a lesson from an expert once a week. He has recently started competing in scholastic chess tournaments, and the mother finds herself swept away by the exciting atmosphere. She finds her own sense of well-being fluctuating with Danny's wins and losses. This woman is a substantial, sensitive, intelligent person and she doesn't want to put an extra burden on her son's shoulders. She is aware of the entity/incremental dynamic and so when Danny loses, she wants to tell him it doesn't matter. But obviously it does matter. He lost and is sad. To tell him it doesn't matter is almost to insult his intelligence. What should she do?

This real-life dynamic has parallels in virtually every field, although we are often our own parent in the moment. How can we balance long-term process with short-term goals and inevitable setbacks? Let's dive in. Danny is an intelligent boy who has decided to dedicate himself for the time being to chess. He loves the challenge of facing off with other young minds and stretching himself to think a little further and more accurately than he could the day before. There is nothing like a worthy opponent to show us our weaknesses and push us to our limit. It is good for Danny to compete, but it is essential that he do so in a healthy manner.

First of all, in the spirit of the previous chapter, Danny's mom can help him internalize a process-first approach by making her everyday feedback respond to effort over results. She should praise good concentration, a good day's work, a lesson learned. When he wins a tournament game, the spotlight should be on the road to that moment and beyond as opposed to the glory. On the other hand, it is okay for a child (or an adult for that matter) to enjoy a win. A parent shouldn't be an automaton, denying the obvious emotional moment to spout platitudes about the long-term learning process when her child is jumping up and down with excitement. When we have worked hard and succeed at something, we should be allowed to smell the roses. The key, in my opinion, is to recognize that the beauty of those roses lies in their transience. It is drifting away even as we inhale. We enjoy the win fully while taking a deep breath, then we exhale, note the lesson learned, and move on to the next adventure.

When Danny loses, the stakes will feel a bit higher. Now he comes out of the tournament room a little teary. He put his heart on the line and lost. How should his mom handle this moment? First of all, she shouldn't say that it doesn't matter, because Danny knows better than that and lying about the situation isolates Danny in his pain. If it didn't matter, then why should he try to win? Why should he study chess and waste their weekends at tournaments? It matters and Danny knows that. So empathy is a good place to start.

I think this mother should give her son a hug. If he is crying, let him cry on her shoulder. She should tell him how proud of him she is. She can tell Danny that it is okay to be sad, that she understands and that she loves him. Disappointment is a part of the road to greatness. When a few moments pass, in a quiet voice, she can ask Danny if he knows what happened in the game. Hopefully the language between parent and child will already be established so Danny knows his mom is asking about psychology, not chess moves (almost all mistakes have both technical and mental components—the chess lessons should be left for after the tournament, when Danny and his teacher study the games). Did he lose his concentration? Did he fall into a downward spiral and make a bunch of mistakes in a row? Was he overconfident? Impatient? Did he get psyched out by a trash talker? Was he tired? Danny will have an idea about his psychological slip, and taking on that issue will be a short-term goal in the continuing process—introspective thinking of this nature can be a very healthy coping mechanism. Through these dialogues, Danny will learn that every loss is an opportunity for growth. He will become increasingly astute psychologically and sensitive to bad habits.

A heartfelt, empathetically present, incrementally inspiring mom or dad or coach can liberate an ambitious child to take the world by the horns. As adults, we have to take responsibility for ourselves and nurture a healthy, liberated mind-set. We need to put ourselves out there, give it our all, and reap the lesson, win or lose. The fact of the matter is that there will be nothing learned from any challenge in which we don't try our hardest. Growth comes at the point of resistance. We learn by pushing ourselves and finding what really lies at the outer reaches of our abilities.

* * *

As I matured as a chess player, there were constantly leaps into the unknown. Because of my growth curve, my life was like that hermit crab who never fits into the same shell for more than a few days. I would have to learn esoteric, initially uncomfortable types of chess positions. I would take on dangerous new rivals who recently emigrated from Eastern Europe or the Soviet Union. I'd travel to distant countries to compete and need to adapt to the alien cultural and chessic customs on the spur of the moment.

I remember when I was eleven years old I went to Timisoara, Romania to represent America in the World Championship for everyone under the age of twelve. Each country sends their champion, and we go to battle. My dad and I had trouble finding the competition site on the opening day and I arrived late to the first round. When I finally got to my seat across from the National Champion of Qatar, there were thirty minutes already off my clock—a large disadvantage. To make matters worse, I didn't recognize any pieces on the chessboard. The untraditional chess set the Romanians had chosen for the tournament was completely bizarre to me. I was sitting in front of a game I had never seen before—like one of my childhood nightmares where I couldn't remember how to move the pieces and cameras were flashing in my face. The moment was quite alarming.

It turns out that I handled the situation pretty well. I took a few deep breaths, made my opening move, and played somewhere between blindfold and looking at the board. Chess was in my blood even if that set was not. I moved quickly to catch up on the clock, calculated in my head as I had done so often in training, and won that first round without much trouble. Then I spent much of the evening getting used to the chess pieces and had an excellent tournament over the next two weeks.

One of the more emotional movements in my young life came as I was turning eleven years old and had to make the painful transition away from my first teacher, Bruce Pandolfini. I loved Bruce, he was part of my family, but I was improving quickly and he just wasn't a strong enough player to keep on coaching me. Bruce was a National Master who hadn't been active in tournaments in years, and I was already approaching his level. We found a wonderful new coach, Chilean International Master Victor Frias, who in time would become a very dear friend of my family. Breaking from Bruce felt like losing a part of myself.

That same year, my father's brutally honest book *Searching for Bobby Fischer* was released around the world. It was a beautifully written account of our journey together during my rise to winning my first national title and years later it would inspire the Paramount film of the same name. I was already well-known in the chess world, but now I was really out there, which put some extra pressure on my shoulders. I went on all the television shows with my awkward adolescent afro and goofy smile. Jane Pauley on *The Today Show* asked me whether I wanted to be like Bobby Fischer. Just then the music started playing, which meant I had five seconds to answer, and I knew Bobby Fischer was crazy so I came out with the brilliant closer: "No, I never want to be like Bobby Fischer, *again.*" Again? What is this kid talking about?

I was having a great time and was just innocent enough to avoid being messed up by the spotlight. I dove deeper and deeper into chess. Of course there were plateaus, periods when my results leveled off while I internalized the information necessary for my next growth spurt, but I didn't mind. I had a burning love for chess and so I pushed through the rocky periods with a can-do attitude. I became a Chess Master a few days after turning thirteen, beating Fischer's mark of thirteen years five months. People were saying that I was a future World Champion, but I didn't hear them. I was a competitor who knew winning and losing and the hair's breadth between. My rivals didn't care about reputation—they just wanted to crush me and I had to keep it real.

There were a few powerful moments that reinforced my young notion that glory had little to do with happiness or long-term success. I'll never forget walking out of the playing hall of the 1990 Elementary School National Championships after winning the title game. There were over 1,500 competitors at the event, all the strongest young players from around the country. I had just won the whole thing . . . and everything felt normal. I stood in the convention hall looking around. There was no euphoria, no opening of the heavens. The world was the same as it had been a few days before. I was Josh. I had a great mom and dad and a cute little sister Katya who was fun to play with. I loved chess and sports and girls and fishing. When I would go back to school on Monday, my friends would say "Awright!" like they did after hitting a jump shot, and then it would be in the past and we would go play football.

CHAPTER 5

THE SOFT ZONE

"Lose Yourself"

World Junior Chess Championship
Calicut, India
November 1993

I was sixteen years old, sitting at a chessboard in Calicut, India. Sweat dripped down my sides as I battled to stay focused in the sweltering heat. The sun was high, the air still, the room stuffed with rustling world-class thinkers. I had traveled from New York City to represent America in the World Championship for chess players under the age of twenty-one. Each country sent its national champion to compete in a grueling two-week marathon of pure concentration, endurance, calculation, strategy—all-out psychological war. My father and I had flown into Bombay a week earlier and had traveled south to the event, where I met my girlfriend, who was representing Slovenia in the women's division of the tournament. She was a brilliant girl, gorgeous, otherworldly, fiercely intense, moody, my first love. Tormented love and war, a complicated mix. Less than ideal for World Championship competition, but the life of a top chess player is a strange one. Brutal competition mixes with intense *friendships. Players try to destroy their opponents, to ruin their lives, and then they reflect on the battle, lick their wounds, cull the lessons, and take a walk.*

From one perspective the opponent is the enemy. On the other hand there is no one who knows you more intimately, no one who challenges you so profoundly or pushes you to excellence and growth so relentlessly. Sitting at a chessboard, just feet away from the other, you can hear every breath, feel each quiver, sense any flicker of fear or exhilaration. Hours pass with your entire being tapping into your opponent's psyche, while the other follows your thoughts like a shadow and yearns for your demise. Brilliant minds all around the world devote themselves to the intense study of this mysterious, brutal intellectual sport, and then the best of them collide in distant outposts.

Here I was, in a strange faraway land, sweating in the oppressive heat, trying to find my beloved art in the figurines in front of me. Above me thousands of spectators hung from the rafters, whispering, staring at the chessboards like Sutra—somehow chess and India resonate like ancient lovers. I was disjointed, out of whack, not yet settled into the rhythm of the tournament. Even for the master, sometimes chess can feel like home, and sometimes it can be completely alienating, a foreign jungle that must be explored as if for the first time. I was trying to find my way home.

Across from me was the Indian National Champion, and between the two of us lay the critical position of our struggle. We were three hours into the battle and I had been thinking for twenty minutes. A curious thing happened in that time. So far I had been grinding my way through this game. It was the first round, I had no flow, no inspired ideas, the pieces were alien, the position strange. After about ten minutes of thought, I began to lose myself in the variations. It is a strange feeling. First you are a person looking at a chessboard. You calculate through the various alternatives, the

mind gaining speed as it pores through the complexities, until con-
sciousness of one's separation from the position ebbs away and what
remains is the sensation of being inside the energetic chess flow. Then
the mind moves with the speed of an electrical current, complex prob-
lems are breezed through with an intuitive clarity, you get deeper
and deeper into the soul of the chess position, time falls away, the
concept of "I" is gone, all that exists is blissful engagement, pure
presence, absolute flow. I was in the zone and then there was an
earthquake.

Everything started to shake and the lights went out. The rafters
exploded with noise, people ran out of the building. I sat still. I
knew what was happening, but I experienced it from within the
chess position. There was a surreal synergy of me and no me, pure
thought and the awareness of a thinker—I wasn't me looking at the
chess position, but I was aware of myself and the shaking world
from within the serenity of pure engagement—and then I solved the
chess problem. Somehow the earthquake and the dying lights spurred
me to revelation. I had a crystallization of thought, resurfaced, and
vacated the trembling playing room. When I returned and play
resumed, I immediately made my move and went on to win the
game.

* * *

This intense moment of my life was the launching point for
my serious investigation of the nuances of performance psychology. I had used an earthquake to reach a higher state of
consciousness and discover a chess solution I may not have
otherwise found. As this book evolves, I will gradually lay
out my current methodology for triggering such states of
creative flow. Eventually, by systematically training oneself,
a competitor can learn how to do this at will. But the first
obstacle I had to overcome as a young chess player was to

avoid being distracted by random, unexpected events—by the mini earthquakes that afflict all of our days. In performance training, first we learn to flow with whatever comes. Then we learn to use whatever comes to our advantage. Finally, we learn to be completely self-sufficient and create our own earthquakes, so our mental process feeds itself explosive inspirations without the need for outside stimulus.

The initial step along this path is to attain what sports psychologists call *The Soft Zone*. Envision the *Zone* as your performance state.*

You are concentrated on the task at hand, whether it be a piece of music, a legal brief, a financial document, driving a car, anything. Then something happens. Maybe your spouse comes home, your baby wakes up and starts screaming, your boss calls you with an unreasonable demand, a truck has a blowout in front of you. The nature of your state of concentration will determine the first phase of your reaction—if you are tense, with your fingers jammed in your ears and your whole body straining to fight off distraction, then you are in a *Hard Zone* that demands a cooperative world for you to function. Like a dry twig, you are brittle, ready to snap under pressure. The alternative is for you to be quietly, intensely focused, apparently relaxed with a serene look on your face, but inside all the mental juices are churning. You flow with whatever comes, integrating every ripple of life into your creative moment. This *Soft Zone* is resilient, like a flexible blade of grass that can move with and survive hurricane-force winds.

---

* The chapter *Building Your Trigger* in Part III of this book, will lay out my methodology for cultivating the ability to enter the zone at will.

Another way of envisioning the importance of the Soft Zone is through an ancient Indian parable that has been quite instructive in my life for many years: A man wants to walk across the land, but the earth is covered with thorns. He has two options—one is to pave his road, to tame all of nature into compliance. The other is to make sandals. Making sandals is the internal solution. Like the Soft Zone, it does not base success on a submissive world or overpowering force, but on intelligent preparation and cultivated resilience.

My relationship to this issue of coping with distraction began with the quirkiness of a ten-year-old boy. In the last chapter I mentioned that as my chess understanding grew more sophisticated and I transitioned to adult tournaments, my games tended to last longer, sometimes going on for six or eight hours. Kids have trouble focusing for so long and strange things can happen to a young mind straining under intense pressure. One day I was working my way through a complex position in a tournament at the Manhattan Chess Club, and a Bon Jovi song I had heard earlier in the day entered my mind. I tried to push it away and return to my calculation, but it just wouldn't leave me alone. At first this seemed funny, but soon the music eclipsed the chess game. I couldn't think, and ended up blundering and losing.

Soon enough, this problem became rampant in my chess life. If I heard a particularly catchy tune at home or on the way to a tournament, I would sometimes be haunted by it for days. This might sound trivial, but for me it was disastrous—there I'd be, eleven years old, facing down a wily old chess master, and the theme song from *Ghostbusters* would be hammering away in my brain. The more I tried to block out the distraction, the louder it would get in my head. As a young boy I felt alone with this problem, but in recent years while lecturing on performance psychology, I have found that many high-stress performers have similar symptoms.

Over time, as I became more and more fixated on irritating mental music, I started being bothered by noises I had never even noticed before. In a silent playing hall, the sound of a distant ambulance or whispering spectators can be an uproar. A ticking chess clock can be a telltale heart, pounding like thunder in your mind. I was having terrible and hilarious noise problems, and then one day I had a breakthrough. I was playing a tournament in Philadelphia with a Phil Collins song rattling away in my brain when I realized that I could think to the beat of the song. My chess calculations began to move to the rhythm of the music, and I played an inspired game. After this moment, I took the bull by the horns and began training to have a more resilient concentration. I realized that in top-rank competition I couldn't count on the world being silent, so my only option was to become at peace with the noise.

The victims of my training method were my parents and sister. A few times a week, while studying chess in my bedroom, I blasted music. Sometimes it was music I liked, sometimes music I didn't like. For a period of many months I blared booming Gyuto monk chants, which drove my sister, Katya, to utter distraction. My family's little apartment was besieged by my bizarre training concept, and it's amazing they put up with me. My idea was to become at peace with distraction, whatever it was. During this period of time, in my early teens, I frequented chess shops near my home and played speed chess in clouds of smoke, which I have always hated. Of course I also played in Washington Square Park, where consistent kibitzing and a steady stream of chess banter is part of the game. There was no blocking out the noise or smoke, and my only option was to integrate my environment into my creative process. So if Bon Jovi was playing, I might be prone to play a bit more aggressively than when I had on quiet classical music. The Gyuto monk chants pounded me into fascinating chessic discoveries. Voices in the park inspired me as they had when I was a young boy. The smoke I learned to live with.

As I turned fourteen and then fifteen years old, my Soft Zone training was really put to the test. The competition for the top of the American scholastic chess ranking was stiffened by a tremendous influx of Soviet immigrants. As the Soviet Union fell apart, many of the powerful Russian players looked for opportunity in the west. These kids were highly trained, excellent fighters, who had been schooled in the famous Pioneers' Palaces of Moscow and Leningrad.* Many of these new rivals were armed with a repertoire of psychological "tricks" that presented serious challenges.

One of the more interesting tactics was implemented by a Russian boy whom I had trouble with for a period of months before I caught on to his game. He was a very strong player so our clashes were always tense, but for some reason I tended to make careless errors against him in the critical positions. Then one day, an old Bulgarian Master named Rudy Blumenfeld approached my father in the Marshall Chess Club and asked him if we were aware of what this boy was doing to me. We were not. He explained that in the climactic moments of the struggle, when I had to buckle

---

*Pioneers' Palaces were state-funded youth centers in the U.S.S.R. in which dedicated children were trained in specific disciplines. These schools were famous for pumping out highly professionalized young chess players. Most Pioneers' Palaces were shut down with the fall of the Soviet Union.

down and patiently work my way through the complications to find a precise solution, this boy would start to tap a chess piece on the side of the table, barely audible, but at a pace that entered and slightly quickened my mental process. This subtle tactic was highly effective and I later found out that it was an offspring of the Soviet study of hypnosis and mind control. The next time we played, I was on the lookout for the tapping and sure enough, in the critical moment it was right there. Hilarious. Once I was aware of what was happening, I was able to turn the tables in our rivalry.

Some of the other young Russian players were far less subtle, and had "tricks" that crossed the borders of sporting ethics. One of these boys, who was my archrival for years, had the habit of kicking me under the table during the critical moments of a game. He would also get up from the board at tournaments and talk about the position in Russian with his coach, a famous Grandmaster. There were complaints, but little was done to stop the cheating. No one could prove what was discussed because of the language barrier, and the truth is that it didn't even matter. While valuable chess ideas might have been exchanged, the psychological effect was much more critical. Opponents felt helpless and wronged—they took on the mentality of victim and so half the battle was already lost. More than once, I watched top young American players reduced to tears by this kid—but these dirty tactics were not reserved for local soil.

In 1993, when we were sixteen, this Russian boy and I both traveled to India to jointly represent America in the World Under 21 Championship and a formal protest was lodged against the American team by seven or eight delegations because he was blatantly cheating at the event. Competitors from all over the world approached me and demanded to know how the Americans could do such a thing. I was embarrassed to be associated with this kid and his seedy repertoire.

As a result of this shift of tone in the U.S. scholastic scene, many of my American contemporaries became dispirited and quit the game. The Russian kids were great players who presented a whole new set of challenges, and instead of adapting and raising their games, American kids dropped out. For my part, the new crew of brilliant Machiavellian rivals made me buckle down. I had my home turf to defend and the first step would be to learn how to handle dirty opponents without losing my cool. Sometimes noticing the psychological tactic was enough to render it harmless—but in the case of the kicking and barefaced cheating, I really had to take on my emotions. These breaks from etiquette were outrageous in the chess world and I was appalled. The problem is that when I got angry, I was thrown off my game. I tried to stay level-headed, but this one rival of mine had no limits. He would push me to the point of utter exasperation and I would often self-destruct.

I have come to believe that the solution to this type of situation does not lie in denying our emotions, but in learning to use them to our advantage. Instead of stifling myself, I needed to channel my mood into heightened focus—and I can't honestly say that I figured out how to do this consistently until years into my martial arts career when dirty opponents tried to take out my knees, target the groin, or head-butt me in the nose in competition.*

---

*See the chapters *Using Adversity* in Part II of the book and *Building Your Trigger* in Part III.

My whole life I have worked on this issue. Mental resilience is arguably the most critical trait of a world-class performer, and it should be nurtured continuously. Left to my own devices, I am always looking for ways to become more and more psychologically impregnable. When uncomfortable, my instinct is not to avoid the discomfort but to become at peace with it. When injured, which happens frequently in the life of a martial artist, I try to avoid painkillers and to change the sensation of pain into a feeling that is not necessarily negative. My instinct is always to seek out challenges as opposed to avoiding them.

This type of internal work can take place in the little moments of our lives. I mentioned how my style over the board was to create chessic mayhem and then to sort my way through the chaos more effectively than my opponents. This was a muscle I built up by training myself to be at peace with the unclear and tumultuous—and most of the training was in everyday life. For example, since my teens, when I play cards, say gin rummy, I rarely arrange my hand. I leave the melds all over the place and do the organization in my head. I've never been a neat guy by nature, and I furthered my messiness for years by consciously leaving my living area chaotic so I could practice organizing things mentally and being mellow in the madness.

Of course this process is never complete. As I am writing this section, a lawn mower just went into gear right outside. A few minutes ago I got up to close the window, but then I sat back down and left it open. The irony was too thick.

CHAPTER 6

The Downward Spiral

Beginning when I was eighteen years old, I spent four years coaching a group of talented young chess students at Public School 116 in New York City. The class usually consisted of about fifteen children, but the core of the team was a group of six second-graders, all friends, all enthusiastic, spirited learners whose rowdiness was offset by a passion for chess. I loved those kids. We had wonderful times as I watched them grow, and eventually the team became city champions, state champions, placed second in the kindergarten through fifth grade National Championship in 1999, and two of them won individual national titles. I'm sure that over the years I learned as much from those kids as they learned from me. There was something so refreshing in seeing their innate, unsullied curiosity in contrast to the material ambition that moved most of my older chess rivals.

One idea I taught was the importance of regaining presence and clarity of mind after making a serious error. This is a hard lesson for all competitors and performers. The first mistake rarely proves disastrous, but the downward spiral of the second, third, and fourth error creates a devastating chain reaction. Any sports fan has seen professional football, basketball, and baseball games won and lost because of a shift in psychological advantage. People speak about momentum as if it were an entity of its own, an unpredictable player on the field, and from my own competitive experience, I can vouch for it seeming that way. The key is to bring that player onto your team by riding the psychological wave when it is behind you, and snapping back into a fresh presence when your clarity of mind begins to be swept away.

With young chess players, the downward spiral dominates competitive lives. In game after game, beginners fall to pieces after making the first mistake. With older, more accomplished players the mistakes are subtler, but the pattern of error begetting error remains true and deadly. Imagine yourself in the following situation:

You are a highly skilled chess Master in the middle of a critical tournament game and you have a much better position. For the last three hours you have been pressuring your opponent, increasing the tension, pushing him closer to the edge, and searching for the decisive moment when your advantage will be converted into a win. Then you make a subtle error that allows your opponent to equalize the position. There is nothing wrong with equality, but you have developed a powerful emotional attachment to being in control of the game. Your heart starts to pound because of the disconcerting chasm between what was and what is.

Chess players are constantly calculating variations and either accepting or dismissing them based on a comparison of how they evaluate the visualized position vs. the original position. So if you have an advantage, make an error, and then still cling to the notion that you have an advantage, then when you calculate a variation that looks equal, you will reject that line of thought because you incorrectly believe it is moving you in the wrong direction. What results is a downward spiral where the foundering player rejects variations he should accept, pushing, with hollow overconfidence, for more than there is. At a high level, pressing for wins in equal positions often results in losing.

As a competitor I've come to understand that the distance between winning and losing is minute, and, moreover, that there are ways to steal wins from the maw of defeat. All great performers have learned this lesson. Top-rate actors often miss a line but improvise their way back on track. The audience rarely notices because of the perfect ease with which the performer glides from troubled waters into the tranquility of the script. Even more impressively, the truly great ones can make the moment work for them, heightening performance with improvisations that shine with immediacy and life. Musicians, actors, athletes, philosophers, scientists, writers understand that brilliant creations are often born of small errors. Problems set in if the performer has a brittle dependence on the safety of absolute perfection or duplication. Then an error triggers fear, detachment, uncertainty, or confusion that muddies the decision-making process.

I often told my wonderful young students to beware of the downward spiral. I taught them that being present at critical moments of competitions can turn losses into wins, and I conveyed strategies for how to do this. Sometimes all the kids needed was to take two or three deep breaths or splash cold water on their faces to snap out of bad states of mind. Other times, more dramatic actions were called for— if I felt dull during a difficult struggle, I would occasionally leave the playing hall and sprint fifty yards outside. This may have seemed strange to spectators, but it served as a complete physiological flushing, and I returned, albeit a bit sweaty, in a brand-new state of mind.

As an eighteen-year-old, I had not yet refined my methodology for snapping into pure presence—this system is the subject of the chapter, *Building Your Trigger*, in Part III—but I understood that avoiding the ripple effect of compounding errors had broad application. Then something happened in my life that drove this rule into my soul.

It was my habit to walk the two miles to P.S. 116 every Wednesday, planning my class and enjoying the city. One fall afternoon I was strolling east along 33rd Street, lost in thought and headed toward the school. Everyone who has grown up in Manhattan knows that it is important to look both ways before crossing the street. Cars run lights and bicyclists ride the wrong way down one-way streets. Drivers are used to narrowly avoiding bustling midtown crowds, and most New Yorkers are untroubled by the cacophony of sirens, blaring horns, and taxis speeding ten inches in front of our noses. Things usually flow nicely, but the margin for error is slim.

There I stood, within the maelstrom of the midtown rush, waiting for the light and thinking about the ideas that I would soon be discussing with my students. A pretty young woman stood a few feet away from me, wearing headphones and moving to the music. I noticed her because I could hear the drumbeat. She wore a grey knee-length skirt, a black sweater, and the typical Manhattan office worker's white sneakers for the trek home. Suddenly she stepped right into the oncoming traffic. I guess she was confused by the chaotic one-way street, because I remember her looking the wrong way down Broadway. Immediately, as she stepped forward, looking right, a bicycle bore down on her from the left. The biker lurched away at the last second and gave her a solid but harmless bump. In my memory, time stops right here. This was the critical moment in the woman's life. She could have walked away unscathed if she had just stepped back onto the pavement, but instead she turned and cursed the fast-pedaling bicyclist.

I can see her now, standing with her back to the traffic on 33rd and Broadway, screaming at the now-distant biker who had just performed a miracle to avoid smashing into her. The image is frozen in my mind. A taxicab was the next to speed around the corner. The woman was struck from behind and sent reeling ten feet into the air. She smashed into a lamppost and was knocked out and bleeding badly. The ambulance and police came and eventually I moved on to P.S. 116, hoping that she would survive.

As I walked into the school, dumbstruck by the severity of what I had just witnessed, I felt compelled to share a version of the story with my students. I left out the gravity of her injuries but I linked life and chess in a way that appeared to move them—this tragedy needn't have happened. I explained how this woman's first mistake was looking the wrong way and stepping into the street in front of traffic. Maybe wearing headphones put her in her own world, a little removed from the immediacy of the moment. Then the biker should have been a wake-up call. She wasn't hurt, but instead of reacting with alertness, she was spooked into anger, irritated that her quiet had been shattered. Her reaction was a perfect parallel to the chess player's downward spiral—after making an error, it is so easy to cling to the emotional comfort zone of what was, but there is also that unsettling sense that things have changed for the worse. The clear thinker is suddenly at war with himself and flow is lost. I have always visualized two lines moving parallel to one another in space. One line is time, the other is our perception of the moment. I showed my students these lines with my hands, moving through the air. When we are present to what is, we are right up front with the expansion of time, but when we make a mistake and get frozen in what was, a layer of detachment builds. Time goes on and we stop. Suddenly we are living, playing chess, crossing the street with our eyes closed in memory. And then comes the taxicab. That chess lesson was surely the most emotional I've ever taught.

Three years later, my students and I traveled to the National Championships in Knoxville, Tennessee. The kids were now in fifth grade and one of the strongest teams in the country. In the final round of the tournament, we were tied for first place. I waited outside the tournament room with the parents of my kids. I always felt strange at a big game if I wasn't the one competing, but after years of teaching children and watching them grow into dynamic competitors, it felt especially harrowing to sit and wait for the verdict. Such experiences taught me that my father was not so misguided when he insisted that watching was more stressful than competing.

So I waited for my students to emerge, joyous or distraught. Out came Ian Ferguson, a thoughtful boy with a wonderful introspective sensitivity and an eccentric talent for the game. He had won his game and he ran over to me, we high-fived, and he said, "You know, Josh, I almost lost." Ian had a giddy, relieved expression on his face, but he also looked like he had seen a ghost. "I made a big mistake and hung my bishop. My opponent laughed and I got really upset and reached for my queen. I was about to move but then I remembered the woman and the bike!"

The move Ian was about to play would have lost his queen and the game, but suddenly he remembered the lesson learned as a seven-year-old. He took a few deep breaths to clear his mind, came back to the moment, collected himself, and won a critical game in the National Championships.

CHAPTER 7

Changing Voice

When the film *Searching for Bobby Fischer* came out I was sixteen years old and winning everything in sight. I became America's youngest International Master that year, I won the U.S. Under 21 Championship twice at sixteen and seventeen, and I came within a hair's breadth of winning the World Under 18 Championship when I was seventeen. From the outside I may have looked unbeatable, but inside I was a kid barely holding everything together.

While I adjusted to the glare of the media spotlight, my relationship to chess was slowly becoming less organic. I found myself playing to live up to Hollywood expectations instead of for love of the game. I understood the danger of becoming distracted by the adulation and I fought to keep focused. But I was slipping. More and more fans came to my tournaments to watch me play and get autographs. Beautiful girls smiled and handed me their phone numbers. Grandmasters smirked and tried to tear off my head. I was living in two worlds, and I started having a peculiar sensation of detachment during tournament games. Sometimes I seemed to play chess from across the room, while watching myself think.

Around the same time I began training with a Russian Grandmaster who urged me to become more conservative stylistically. He was a lovely man—literary, compassionate, funny—as human beings we connected but chessically we didn't gel. He was a systematic strategist with a passion for slow, subtle maneuvering. I had always been a creative, attacking player who loved the wild side of chess. I liked to live on the edge in the spirit of Bobby Fischer and Garry Kasparov, and now my new coach had me immerse myself in the opposite sensibility. We dove into the great prophylactic players, studying the games of Tigran Petrosian and Anatoly Karpov, ex-world champions who seemed to breathe a different air. Instead of creating exciting dynamics in their positions, these guys competed like Anacondas, preempting every aggressive idea until opponents were paralyzed and gasping for life.

While I found this work interesting, the effects of moving away from my natural voice as a competitor were disturbing. Instead of following my instincts, my coach urged me to ask myself, "What would Karpov do here?" But Karpov had cold blood and mine boiled. When he searched for tiny strategic advantages, I yearned for wild dynamics. As I tried to play in the style that pleased my coach, chess began to feel alien. At times I felt as though my head was in a thick cloud and I couldn't see the variations. My strengths as a young champion—consistency, competitive presence, focus, drive, passion, creativity—were elusive and moving out of reach. I still loved chess, but it no longer felt like an extension of my being.

Of course I was also at that moment when boys become men. While my chess life was growing increasingly complex, I was thriving in my coming of age. My last two years of high school were spent at the Professional Children's School, an exciting learning environment teeming with brilliant young actors, dancers, musicians, a fencer, a young entrepreneur, a couple of gymnasts, and now a chess player. Everyone at PCS was pursuing something and many students were famous from movie careers or Broadway roles (talent shows and school plays were absolute jaw-droppers). The school gave me more flexibility to catch up on my studies after traveling to distant tournaments, and the education was first rate—one creative writing class with a brilliant woman named Shellie Sclan was the most inspiring academic experience of my life.

I read Hemingway, Dostoevsky, Hesse, Camus, and Jack Kerouac. I went out with girls and brooded about spending half my life entrenched over a chessboard trying to will heart and soul out of sixty-four squares. Socially, PCS allowed young celebrities to insulate themselves from staring fans, because everyone was exceptional in one way or another. This was a tremendous relief and I thrived at PCS; but in my professional life I felt oppressed. The one-two punch of a fame I wasn't really prepared for and a building sense of alienation from the art I loved had me hungering for escape. When I graduated from high school, I deferred my acceptance at Columbia University and took off for Eastern Europe. I had fallen in love with a Slovenian girl and decided to spend some time on the road.

This was an intense, formative period of my life. As I matured into a nineteen- and twenty-year-old young man, my relationship to chess was infused with a more sophisticated consciousness. I was no longer soaring with the momentum of my early career. Now I had my demons to wrestle with. Self-doubt and alienation were part of my reality, but in Europe I was free of the immense pressures of my celebrity back home.

I studied chess and literature and traveled the world with my notebook and a rucksack. My home base was a little village called Vrholvje, nestled in the mountains of southern Slovenia and overlooking northern Italy. I lived romantically, took long walks in the woods, and dove deeper and deeper into chess, sifting through the hidden nuances of nine rounds I had just played against Grandmasters in Amsterdam, Crete, or Budapest. Then, after periods of intense work, I would take off for another big tournament in some faraway place.

During these years I discovered a powerful new private relationship to chess. I worked on the game tirelessly, but was now moved less by ambition than by a yearning for self-discovery. While my understanding of the game deepened, I continued to be uneven and, at times, self-defeating in competition. I was consistently unhappy before leaving for tournaments, preferring my lifestyle of introspection and young romance. When I dragged myself off to tournaments, some days I would play brilliant chess and others I would feel disconnected, like a poet without his muse. In order to make my new knowledge manifest over the board, I had to figure out how to release myself from the baggage I had acquired, and I developed a method of study that made chess and life begin to merge in my being.

At this point in my career, despite my issues, I was still a strong chess player competing against world-class rivals. Each tournament game was riddled with intricate complications and hour upon hour of mounting tension. My opponents and I created increasingly subtle problems for the other to solve, building the pressure in the position until the chessboard and the mind itself felt like a fault line, trembling, on the verge of explosion. Sometimes technical superiority proved decisive, but more often somebody cracked, as if a tiny weakness deep in the being suddenly erupted onto the board.

These moments, where the technical and psychological collide, are where I directed my study of the game. In the course of a nine-round chess tournament, I'd arrive at around four or five critical positions that I didn't quite understand or in which I made an error. Immediately after each of my games, I quickly entered the moves into my computer, noting my thought process and how I felt emotionally at various stages of the battle. Then after the tournament, armed with these fresh impressions, I went back to Vrholvje and studied the critical moments.

This was the work that I referred to in the Introduction as *numbers to leave numbers.* Usually long study sessions went like this: I began with the critical position from one of my games, where my intuitive understanding had not been up to the challenge. At first my mind was like a runner on a cold winter morning—stiff, unhappy about the coming jog, dreary. Then I began to move, recalling my attacking ideas in the struggle and how nothing had fully connected. I tried to pick apart my opponent's position and discovered new layers of his defensive resources, all the while my mind thawing, integrating the evolving structural dynamics it had not quite understood before. Over time my blood started flowing, sweat came, I settled into the rhythm of analysis, soaked in countless patterns of evolving sophistication as I pored over what a computer would consider billions of variations. Like a runner in stride, my thinking became unhindered, free-flowing, faster and faster as I lost myself in the position. Sometimes the study would take six hours in one sitting, sometimes thirty hours over a week. I felt like I was living, breathing, sleeping in that maze, and then, as if from nowhere, all the complications dissolved and I understood.

When I looked at the critical position from my tournament game, what had stumped me a few days or hours or weeks before now seemed perfectly apparent. I saw the best move, felt the correct plan, understood the evaluation of the position. I couldn't explain this new knowledge with variations or words. It felt more elemental, like rippling water or a light breeze. My chess intuition had deepened. This was the study of *numbers to leave numbers.* *

A fascinating offshoot of this method of analysis was that I began to see connections between the leaps of chess understanding and my changing vision of the world. During my study of the critical positions, I noted the *feeling* I had during the actual chess game. I explained above how in the pressure of tournaments, the tension in the mind mounts with the tension in the position, and an error on the board usually parallels a psychological collapse of sorts. Almost invariably, there was a consistent psychological strain to my errors in a given tournament, and what I began to notice

---

*It is important to understand that by *numbers to leave numbers,* or *form to leave form,* I am describing a process in which technical information is integrated into what feels like natural intelligence. Sometimes there will literally be numbers. Other times there will be principles, patterns, variations, techniques, ideas. A good literal example of this process, one that does in fact involve numbers, is a beginner's very first chess lesson. All chess players learn that the pieces have numerical equivalents—bishops and knights are worth three pawns, a rook is five pawns, a queen is nine. Novices are counting in their heads or on their fingers before they make exchanges. In time, they will stop counting. The pieces will achieve a more flowing and integrated value system. They will move across the board like fields of force. What was once seen mathematically is now felt intuitively.

is that my problems on the chessboard usually were manifesting themselves in my life outside of chess.

For example, while living in Slovenia it appealed to my sense of adventure to be on the road, traveling, writing, exploring new places, but I also missed my family. I hardly ever spoke English, communicating with everyone but my girlfriend (who did speak English) in broken Spanish, bad Italian, and even worse Serbo-Croatian. I was a stranger in a strange land. On the other hand, I felt quite at home in Vrholvje. I loved the charming village life, and enjoyed my periods of introspection. But then every month or so I would leave Slovenia and take off, alone, for Hungary, Germany, or Holland to compete in a grueling two-week tournament. Each trip was an adventure, but in the beginning I was invariably homesick. I missed my girlfriend. I missed my family, I missed my friends, I missed everything. I felt like a leaf in the wind, adrift, all alone. The first few days were always rough but then I'd get my bearings in the new city and have a wonderful time. I was just having trouble with transitions.

It was amazing how clearly this manifested on the chessboard. For a period of time, almost all my chess errors came in a moment immediately following or preceding a big change. For example, if I was playing a positional chess game, with complex maneuvering, long-term strategical planning, and building tension, and suddenly the struggle exploded into concrete tactics, I would sometimes be slow to accommodate the new scenario. Or, if I was playing a very tactical position that suddenly transformed into an abstract endgame, I would keep on calculating instead of taking a deep breath and making long-term plans. I was having trouble with the first major decision following the departure from prepared opening analysis and I was not keeping pace with sudden shifts in momentum. My whole chess psychology was about holding on to what was, because I was fundamentally homesick. When I finally noticed this connection, I tackled transitions in both chess and life. In chess games, I would take some deep breaths and clear my mind when the character of the struggle shifted. In life, I worked on embracing change instead of fighting it. With awareness and action, in both life and chess my weakness was transformed into a strength.

Once I recognized that deeply buried secrets in a competitor tend to surface under intense pressure, my study of chess became a form of psychoanalysis. I unearthed my subtlest foibles through chess, and the link between my personal and artistic sides was undeniable. The psychological theme could range from transitions to resilient concentration, fluidity of mind, control, leaps into the unknown, sitting with tension, the downward spiral, being at peace with discomfort, giving into fatigue, emotional turbulence, and invariably the chess moves paralleled the life moment. Whenever I noticed a weakness, I took it on.

I also studied my opponents closely. Like myself, their psychological nuances in life manifested over the board. I would watch a rival tapping his feet impatiently while waiting for an elevator or carefully maneuvering around his peas on a dinner plate. If someone was a controlling person who liked to calculate everything out before acting, I would make the chess position chaotic, beyond calculation, so he would have to make that uncomfortable leap into the unknown. If an opponent was intuitive, fast, and hungering for abstract creations, I would make the position precise, so the only solution lay in patient, mind-numbing math.

When I was twenty-one years old and came back to America, I was more in love with the study of chess than ever. The game had become endlessly fascinating to me, and its implications stretched far beyond winning and losing—I was no longer primarily refining the skill of playing chess, but was discovering myself through chess. I saw the art as a movement closer and closer to an unattainable truth, as if I were traveling through a tunnel that continuously deepened and widened as I progressed. The more I knew about the game, the more I realized how much there was to know. I emerged from each good work session in slightly deeper awe of the mystery of chess, and with a building sense of humility. Increasingly, I felt more tender about my work than fierce. Art was truly becoming for art's sake.

Of course not everything was fine and dandy. While personal growth had been my focus in my life on the road, when I came back to America I was back in the limelight. Fans once again mobbed me at tournaments, and I was expected to perform—but I was in one of those vulnerable stages of growth, like the hermit crab between shells. While my new philosophical approach to chess was exciting spiritually, it was also a bit undermining for a young competitor. The youthful arrogance of believing I had the answers was gone. I was flexible and introspective but lacked that unique character and drive to my game that had made me a champion. As a lover and learner of chess, I was flying, but as an artist and performer I was all locked up.

CHAPTER 8

BREAKING STALLIONS

I think a life of ambition is like existing on a balance beam. As a child, there is no fear, no sense for the danger of falling. The beam feels wide and stable, and natural playfulness allows for creative leaps and fast learning. You can run around doing somersaults and flips, always testing yourself with a love for discovery and new challenges. If you happen to fall off—no problem, you just get back on. But then, as you get older, you become more aware of the risk of injury. You might crack your head or twist your knee. The beam is narrow and you have to stay up there. Plunging off would be humiliating.

While a child can make the beam a playground, high-stress performers often transform the beam into a tightrope. Any slip becomes a crisis. Suddenly you have everything to lose, the rope is swaying above a crater of fire, increasingly dramatic acrobatics are expected of you but the air feels thick with projectiles aimed to dislodge your balance. What was once light and inspiring can easily mutate into a nightmare.

A key component of high-level learning is cultivating a resilient awareness that is the older, conscious embodiment of a child's playful obliviousness. My chess career ended with me teetering on a string above leaping flames, and in time, through a different medium, I rediscovered a relationship to ambition and art that has allowed me the freedom to create like a child under world championship pressure. This journey, from child back to child again, is at the very core of my understanding of success.

I believe that one of the most critical factors in the transition to becoming a conscious high performer is the degree to which your relationship to your pursuit stays in harmony with your unique disposition. There will inevitably be times when we need to try new ideas, release our current knowledge to take in new information—but it is critical to integrate this new information in a manner that does not violate who we are. By taking away our natural voice, we leave ourselves without a center of gravity to balance us as we navigate the countless obstacles along our way. It might be interesting to examine, with a bit more detail, how this happened to me.

* * *

Mark Dvoretsky and Yuri Razuvaev are the pillars of the Russian school of chess. Considered by many to be the two greatest chess trainers in the world, these two men have devoted their lives to carving talented young chess masters into world-class competitors. They are both armed with an enormous repertoire of original educational material for top-caliber players and you would be hard-pressed to find a Grandmaster out there who was not seriously influenced by one of them. Between the ages of sixteen and twenty-one, I had the opportunity to work extensively with both of these legendary coaches and I believe the implications of their diametrically opposed pedagogical styles are critical for students of all endeavors. They were certainly critical for me.

When you meet Yuri Razuvaev, you feel calmed. He has the humble, peaceful air of a Buddhist monk and a sweet, slightly ironic smile. If making a decision, for example about where to eat, he will shrug and gently imply that both possibilities would find him quite content. His language is similarly abstract. His mildest comments feel like natural koans, and in conversation it is all too easy to let gems slip through your mind like a breeze. When the chessboard comes out, Razuvaev's face settles into a relaxed focus, his eyes become piercing, and a razor-sharp mind comes to bear. Analyzing with Razuvaev, I consistently felt as though he was penetrating the deepest wrinkles in my mind through my every chess move. After just a few hours of work with him, I had the impression he understood me more truly than almost anybody in my life. It was like playing chess with Yoda.

Mark Dvoretsky is a very different type of personality. I believe he is the most important author for chess professionals in the world. His books are extensive training programs for world-class players and are studied religiously by strong International Masters and Grandmasters. "Reading" a Dvoretsky book takes many months of hard work, because they are so densely packed with ideas about some of the more esoteric elements of serious chess thinking. It's amazing how many hundreds of hours I spent laboring my way through Dvoretsky's chapters, my brain pushed to the limit, emerging from every study session utterly exhausted, but infused with a slightly more nuanced understanding of the outer reaches of chessic potential. On the page, the man is a genius.

In life, Dvoretsky is a tall, heavyset man who wears thick glasses and rarely showers or changes his clothes. He is socially awkward and when not talking about or playing chess, he seems like a big fish flopping on sand. I met Dvoretsky at the first Kasparov-Karpov World Championship match in Moscow when I was seven years old, and we studied together sporadically throughout my teens. He would occasionally live in my family's home for four or five days at a time when he visited America. During these periods, it seemed that every concern but chess was an intrusive irrelevance. When we were not studying, he would sit in his room, staring at chess positions on his computer. At meals, he would mumble while dropping food on the floor, and in conversation thick saliva collected at the corners of his mouth and often shot out like streams of glue. If you have read Nabokov's wonderful novel *The Defense,* about the eccentric chess genius Luzhin—well, that is Dvoretsky.

When seated at a chessboard, Dvoretsky comes to life. His thick fingers somehow manipulate the pieces with elegance. He is extremely confident, arrogant in fact. He is most at home across the table from a talented pupil, and immediately begins setting up enormously complex chess compositions for the student to solve. His repertoire of abstruse material seems limitless, and it keeps on coming hour after hour in relentless interrogation. Dvoretsky loves to watch gifted chess minds struggle with his problems. He basks in his power while young champions are slowly drained of their audacious creativity. As a student, I found these sessions to be resonant of Orwell's prison scenes in *1984,* where independently minded thinkers were ruthlessly broken down until all that was left was a shell of a person.

Training with Yuri Razuvaev feels much more like a spiritual retreat than an Orwellian nightmare. Razuvaev's method depends upon a keen appreciation for each student's personality and chessic predispositions. Yuri has an amazing psychological acumen, and his instructional style begins with a close study of his student's chess games. In remarkably short order, he discovers the core of the player's style and the obstructions that are blocking pure self-expression. Then he devises an individualized training program that systematically deepens the student's knowledge of chess while nurturing his or her natural gifts.

Mark Dvoretsky, on the other hand, has created a comprehensive training system that he believes all students should fit into. His method when working with a pupil is to break the student down rather brutally and then stuff him or her into the cookie-cutter mold of his training system. In my opinion this approach can have profoundly negative consequences for spirited young students.

During the critical period of my chess career following the release of the film *Searching for Bobby Fischer,* there was a disagreement about what direction my study should take. On one side was Dvoretsky and his protégé, my full time coach, who believed I should immerse myself in the study of prophylaxis, the art of playing chess like an anaconda. Great prophylactic players, like Karpov and Petrosian, seem to sense their opponent's intention. They systematically cinch down the pressure, squeezing every last breath of life out of their prey while preventing any aggressive attempt before it even begins to materialize. They are counterpunchers by nature and they tend to be quiet, calculating, rather introverted personalities. On the other side of the argument was Yuri Razuvaev, who insisted that I should continue to nurture my natural voice as a chess player. Razuvaev believed that I was a gifted attacking player who should not be bullied away from my strengths. There was no question that I needed to learn more about Karpov's type of chess to make the next steps in my development, but Razuvaev pointed out that I could learn Karpov from Kasparov.

This was a delicate and rather mystical-feeling idea, and I wish I had possessed the sophistication as a sixteen-year-old boy to see its power. On one level, Razuvaev's point was that the great attacking players all possess keen understanding of positional chess, and the way for someone like myself to study high-level positional chess is to study the way the great players *of my nature* have integrated this element of the art. An interesting parallel would be to consider a lifetime rock guitarist who wants to learn about classical music. Let's say there are two possible guides for him in this educational process. One is an esoteric classical composer who has never thought much of the "vulgarity of rock and roll," and another is a fellow rocker who fell in love with classical music years ago and decided to dedicate his life to this different genre of music. The ex-rocker might touch a common nerve while the composer might feel like an alien. I needed to learn Karpov through a musician whose blood boiled just like mine.

Razuvaev's educational philosophy falls very much in line with Taoist teachers who might say "learn this from that" or "learn the hard from the soft." In most everyday life experiences, there seems to be a tangible connection between opposites. Consider how you may not realize how much someone's companionship means to you until they are gone—heartbreak can give the greatest insight into the value of love. Think about how good a healthy leg feels after an extended time on crutches—sickness is the most potent ambassador for healthy living. Who knows water like a man dying of thirst? The human mind defines things in relation to one another—without light the notion of darkness would be unintelligible

Along the same lines, I have found that if we feed the unconscious, it will discover connections between what may appear to be disparate realities. The path to artistic insight in one direction often involves deep study of another—the intuition makes uncanny connections that lead to a crystallization of fragmented notions. The great Abstract Expressionist painters and sculptors, for example, came to their revolutionary ideas through precise realist training. Jackson Pollock could draw like a camera, but instead he chose to splatter paint in a wild manner that pulsed with emotion. He studied form to leave form. And in his work, the absence of classical structure somehow contains the essence of formal training—but without its ritualized limitations.

By extension, studying the greatest attacking chess games ever played, I would inevitably gain a deep appreciation for defensive nuance. Every high-level attacking chess creation emerges from a subtle building of forces that is at the core of positional chess. Just as the yin-yang symbol possesses a kernel of light in the dark, and of dark in the light, creative leaps are grounded in a technical foundation. Years later, my martial arts training would integrate this understanding into my everyday work, but as a teenager I didn't understand. I don't think I was even present to the question.

TWO WAYS OF BREAKING A STALLION

Along with her many other impressive abilities, my mom, Bonnie Waitzkin, trains horses. She used to compete as a hunter jumper and dressage rider, and as a young boy I often went with her to the barn in New Jersey and romped around on the ponies. I could never believe the way she communicated with the animals. If there was a problematic horse, people called my little mom, who would walk up to an angry 1,700-pound stallion, speak in a soothing voice, and soon enough the horse would be in the palm of her hand.

Mom has a unique ability to communicate with all animals. I've seen her hand-line five-hundred-pound blue marlin to the side of the boat, with barely any strength. Angry, barking dogs quiet and lick her legs. Birds flock to her. She is a whisperer. She loves the animals and she speaks their natural body language.

Bonnie explains that there are two basic ways of taming a wild horse. One is to tie it up and freak it out. Shake paper bags, rattle cans, drive it crazy until it submits to any noise. Make it endure the humiliation of being controlled by a rope and pole. Once it is partially submissive, you tack the horse, get on top, spur it, show it who's boss—the horse fights, bucks, twists, turns, runs, but there is no escape. Finally the beast drops to its knees and submits to being domesticated. The horse goes through pain, rage, frustration, exhaustion, to near death . . . then it finally yields. This is the method some like to call *shock and awe*.

Then there is the way of the horse whisperers. My mother

explains, "When the horse is very young, a foal, we gentle it. The horse is always handled. You pet it, feed it, groom it, stroke it, it gets used to you, likes you. You get on it and there is no fight, nothing to fight." So you guide the horse toward doing what you want to do because he wants to do it. You synchronize desires, speak the same language. You don't break the horse's spirit. My mom goes on: "If you walk straight toward a horse, it will look at you and probably run away. You don't have to oppose the horse in that way. Approach indirectly, without confrontation. Even an adult horse can be gentled. Handle him nicely, make your intention the horse's intention.

"Then, when riding, both you and the horse want to maintain the harmony you have established. If you want to move to the right, you move to the right and so the horse naturally moves right to balance your weight." Rider and animal feel like one. They have established a bond that neither wants to disrupt. And most critically, in this relationship between man and beast, the horse has not been whitewashed. When trained, he will bring his unique character to the table. The gorgeous, vibrant spirit is still flowing in an animal that used to run the plains.

* * *

Dvoretsky wanted to break me—*shock and awe*—and Razuvaev wanted to bring out my natural shine. As it was, perhaps because of his own playing style, my full-time coach was drawn to Dvoretsky's conclusions—and so from the age of sixteen a large part of my chess education involved distancing myself from my natural talents and integrating this Karpovian brand of chess. As a result, I lost my center of gravity as a competitor. I was told to ask myself, "What would Karpov play here?" and I stopped trusting my intuition because it was not naturally Karpovian. When the maelstrom surrounding *Searching for Bobby Fischer* hit me, a big part of my struggle holding course stemmed from my sense of alienation from my natural voice as an artist. I lacked an inner compass.

Reflecting back on the last years of my chess career, more than anything else I am struck by the complexity of the issues confronting an artist or competitor on a long-term learning curve. It would be too easy to say that one or two factors were decisive in pushing me away from chess. I could say that the film *Searching for Bobby Fischer* put too much pressure on my shoulders. I could say that a bad teacher distanced me from my natural love for the game. I could say that I discovered happiness elsewhere. But all this would be too simple.

To my mind, the fields of learning and performance are an exploration of greyness—of the in-between. There is the careful balance of pushing yourself relentlessly, but not so hard that you melt down. Muscles and minds need to stretch to grow, but if stretched too thin, they will snap. A competitor needs to be process-oriented, always looking for stronger opponents to spur growth, but it is also important to keep on winning enough to maintain confidence. We have to release our current ideas to soak in new material, but not so much that we lose touch with our unique natural talents. Vibrant, creative idealism needs to be tempered by a practical, technical awareness.

Navigating our way to excellence is tricky. There are shoals on either side of the narrow channel and in my chess career I ran into more than one. The effects of moving away from my natural voice as a competitor were particularly devastating. But with the perspective of time, I understand that I was offered a rare opportunity to grow. Much of what I believe in today has evolved from the brutal testing ground of my final years in chess.

PART II

◆

MY SECOND ART

CHAPTER 9

BEGINNER'S MIND

I first picked up *On the Road* while finishing my preparation for the World Under 18 Chess Championship in Szeged, Hungary, in the summer of 1994. Jack Kerouac's vision was like electricity in my veins. His ability to draw sheer joy from the most mundane experiences opened up the world to me. I felt oppressed by the pressures of my career, but then I'd watch a leaf falling or rain pelting the Hudson River, and I'd be in ecstasies about the raw beauty. I was on fire with a fresh passion for life when I traveled to Hungary.

Over the course of the two-week tournament, I played inspired chess. Entering the final round I was tied for first place with the Russian champion, Peter Svidler. He was an immensely powerful player and is now one of the top Grandmasters in the world, but going into the game I was very confident. He must have felt that, because Svidler offered me a draw after just half an hour of play. All I had to do was shake hands to share the world title—it was unclear who would win on tie-breaks. Shake hands! But in my inimitable leave-it-on-the-field style that has won and lost me many a battle, I declined, pushed for a win, and ended up losing an absolute heartbreaker.

That night I took off across Eastern Europe to visit my girlfriend in a resort village in Slovenia. She was the women's chess champion of her country, and was about to compete in a major tournament. A rucksack on my back, *On the Road* in my lap, I took trains and buses and random car rides, digging it all with a wired energy. I ended up in a little town called Ptuj, and will never forget the sight of Kiti walking toward me on a long dirt road, wearing a red sundress that moved with the breeze and seemed out of character, too soft. As she came closer, her head tilted to the side; in her beauty was something severe, distant, and a chill came over me.

Our relationship was a rocky one, and we ended up fighting for two days straight until I left, exasperated, heartbroken, working my way back around war-torn Croatia to Hungary so I could fly home. I finished *On the Road* in the middle of the Austrian night, sheets of rain pounding down on an old train as it groaned into the darkness, a drunk Russian snoring across the car from me, mixing with the laughs of gypsy children in the compartment next door. My emotional state was bizarre. I had just lost the World Championship and the love of my young life, and I hadn't slept in six days, but I was more alive than ever before.

Three weeks later, I was standing on a Brazilian street corner the day before representing the U.S. in the World Under 21 Championships, and suddenly Kiti was in front of me, smiling, looking into my eyes. We laughed and our adventures continued. Such was my life.

After finishing *On the Road,* I began reading *The Dharma Bums,* Kerouac's fantastic story centering on the Beat Generation's relationship to Zen Buddhism. I believe this was my first real exposure to a (albeit rather eccentric) vision of Buddhist thought. I loved the hedonistic internal journeys and rebellious wisdom of Gary Snyder. I yearned to retreat into the mountains and live with the birds. Instead I went to the Shambhala Center in downtown Manhattan and studied meditation. I tried to chill myself out, sitting cross legged on the floor, focusing on my breath. I had moments of peace, but for the most part I was boiling with a hunger to leave everything behind.

That's when I took off to live in Slovenia, and it was in my European wanderings that I found the Tao Te Ching— an ancient Chinese text of naturalist musings, believed to be written by the hermetic sage Laotse (also known as Lao Tsu) in the 6th century B.C.E. I described earlier how during these years my relationship to chess became increasingly introspective and decreasingly competitive. A large factor in this movement was my deepening connection to Taoist philosophy.

Studying the Tao Te Ching, I felt like I was unearthing everything I sensed but could not yet put into words. I yearned to "blunt my sharpness," to temper my ambitions and make a movement away from the material.* Laotse's focus was inward, on the underlying essence as opposed to the external manifestations. The Tao Te Ching's wisdom centers on releasing obstructions to our natural insight, seeing false constructs for what they are and leaving them behind. This made sense to me aesthetically, as I was already involved with my study of *numbers to leave numbers.* My understanding of learning was about searching for the flow that lay at the heart of, and transcended, the technical. The resonance of these ideas was exciting for me, and turned out to be hugely important later in my life. But for an eighteen-year-old

*Tao Te Ching, chapter 4.

boy, more than anything the Tao Te Ching provided a framework to help me sort out my complicated relationship to material ambition. It helped me figure out what was important apart from what we are told is important.

When I returned to America after my time in Europe, I wanted to learn more about the ideas of ancient China. In October 1998, I walked into William C. C. Chen's Tai Chi Chuan studio on the recommendation of a family friend. Tai Chi is the meditative and martial embodiment of Taoist philosophy, and William C. C. Chen is one of its greatest living masters. The combination was irresistible.

* * *

I think what initially struck me that fall evening, when I watched my first Tai Chi class, was that the goal was not winning, but, simply, being. Each of the twelve people on the dojo floor seemed to be listening to some quiet, internal muse. The group moved together, slowly gliding through what looked like an earthy dance. The teacher, William C. C. Chen, flowed in front of the students, leading the meditation. He was sixty-four years old but in the moment he could have passed for anywhere between forty and eighty, one of those ageless beings who puts out the energy of an ancient gorilla. He moved dreamily, as if he were in a thick cloud. Watching Chen, I had the impression that every fiber of his body was pulsing with some strange electrical connection. His hand pushed through empty space like it was feeling and drawing from the subtlest ripples in the air; profound, precise, nothing extra. His grace was simplicity itself. I sat entranced. I had to learn more.

The next day I went back to the school to take my first class. I remember that as I stepped onto the floor, my skin

prickled with excitement. Everyone was warming up, swaying around with their fists slapping into their lower backs in
what I would later learn was a Qigong exercise. I tried to follow but my shoulders felt tight. Then Chen walked onto the
floor and the room was silent. He smiled gently as he found
his place in front of the class. Then he slowly closed his eyes
while exhaling deeply, his mind moving inward, everything settling into stillness, his whole body becoming
molten and live. I was rapt. From the stillness, his palms
floated up, the simplest movement was profound from this
man, and he began to lead us through the opening postures
of the Tai Chi form. I followed along as best I could. All the
profundity I was struck by in Chen's form combined with a
sense of total befuddlement. His grace was a world away. I
felt stiff and awkward.

After ten minutes Chen broke the class into groups and I
was put with a senior student who patiently described the
basic principles of Tai Chi's body mechanics. As we repeated
the first few movements over and over, I was told to release
my hip joints, breathe into the lower abdomen, relax my
shoulders and back. Relax, relax, relax. I never knew I was so
tense! After years of hunching over a chessboard, my posture
needed serious attention. The man explained that my head
should float as though it were suspended by a string from
the crown point. This felt good.

Over the next few months, I learned the sixty basic movements of the meditative form. I was a beginner, a child
learning to crawl, and the world began to lift off my shoulders.
Chess was irrelevant on these wooden floors. There were no
television cameras, no fans, no suffocating pressure. I practiced for hours every evening. Slowly but surely, the alien
language began to feel natural, a part of me. My previous

attempts at meditation had been tumultuous—a ball of nerves chilling itself out. Now it was as if my insides were being massaged while my mind floated happily through space. As I consciously released the tension from one part of my body at a time, I experienced a surprising sense of physical awareness. A subtle buzzing tickled my fingers. I played with that feeling, and realized that when deeply relaxed, I could focus on any part of my body and become aware of a rich well of sensation that had previously gone unnoticed. This was interesting.

From my first days at the school, my interactions with William Chen were stirring. His teaching style was understated, his body a well of information. He seemed to exist on another wavelength, tapped into a sublime reality that he shared through osmosis. He spoke softly, moved deeply, taught those who were ready to learn. Gems were afterthoughts, hidden beneath the breath, and you could pick them up or not—he hardly seemed to care. I was amazed how much of his subtle instruction went unnoticed.

A beginner class usually had anywhere from three to twenty students, depending on the day or the weather. My favorite sessions were rainy or snowy weekday nights when most people chose to stay home. Then it was just Chen and one or two die-hards, a private lesson. But more often there were ten or so beginners in the room, working out their issues, trying to smooth their movements. Master Chen would stand in front of a large mirror so he could observe the students while leading the class. He would smile and make some little quip about the current squabble between his son and daughter. He was very mortal. No fancy words. No spiritual claims. He didn't expect the bowing and scraping usually associated with Chinese martial arts—"If I can do it, you can do it," was his humble message.

Chen reminded me quite powerfully of Yuri Razuvaev, the Yoda-like Russian chess teacher who had encouraged me to nurture my natural voice. Chen had the same kind of insight into the student, although his wisdom was very physical. I could be doing the form in class, feel a little off, and he would look at me from across the room, tilt his head, and come over. Then he would imitate my posture precisely, point to a leg or a spot on the lower back where there was tension, and demonstrate with his body how to ease the crimp. He was always right. Chen's ability to mimic physical structure down to the smallest detail was amazing. He read the body like a great chess player reads the board. A huge element of Tai Chi is releasing obstructions so the body and mind can flow smoothly together. If there is tension in one place, the mind stops there, and the fluidity is broken. Chen could always see where my mind was.

Over time, as we got to know each other, our interactions became increasingly subtle. He would notice a small hitch in my form like a psychological wrinkle buried deeply in my shoulder, and from across the room, in a blink, he would look into my eyes, take on my structure, make a small adjustment, and then fall back into his own body and move on with the class. I would follow and immediately feel released, as if somebody had taken a heavy knot out of my back. He might glance back to check if I had noticed, he might not. If I was ready, I would learn. It was amazing how many students would miss such rich moments because they were looking at themselves in the mirror or impatiently checking the time. It took full concentration to pick up each valuable lesson, so on many levels Tai Chi class was an exercise in awareness. While this method worked very well for me, it also weeded out students who were not committed to serious practice. I've seen many emerge bored from Chen's most inspiring classes, because they wanted to be spoonfed and did not open their receptors to his subtleties.

A key movement at this stage of my Tai Chi learning experience was the coordination of breath and mind. This relationship is a critical component of Tai Chi Chuan and I think it's important to take a moment to explain. Many Chinese martial arts masters impose a forced, old-school breathing method on their students. The idea is that a particular art has created a superior method of breath control and this method should be followed religiously. William Chen's humble vision of this issue is that breathing should be natural. Or, more accurately, breathing should be a return to what was natural before we got stressed out by years of running around a hectic world and internalizing bad habits. I certainly had plenty of those.

In William Chen's Tai Chi form, expansive (outward or upward) movements occur with an in-breath, so the body and mind wake up, energize into a shape. He gives the example of reaching out to shake the hand of someone you are fond of, waking up after a restful sleep, or agreeing with somebody's idea. Usually, such positive moments are associated with an in-breath—in the Tai Chi form, we "breathe into the fingertips." Then, with the out-breath, the body releases, de-energizes, like the last exhalation before falling asleep.

For a glimmer of this experience, hold your palms in front of you, forefingers a few inches apart, shoulders relaxed. Now breathe in while gently expanding your fingers, putting your mind on your middle fingers, forefingers, and thumbs. Your breath and mind should both softly shoot to the very tips of your fingers. This inhalation is slow, gently pulling oxygen into your *dan tien* (a spot believed to be the energetic center—located two and a half inches below the navel) and then moving that energy from your dan tien to your fingers. Once your inhalation is complete, gently exhale. Release your fingers, let your mind fall asleep, relax your hip joints, let everything sag into soft, quiet awareness. Once exhalation is complete, you reenergize. Try that exercise for a few minutes and see how you feel.

In my experience, when these principles of breathing merge with the movements of the Tai Chi form, practice becomes like the ebb and flow of water meeting a beach, the waves lapping against the sand (in-breath), then the water trickling back out to sea (gentle, full exhalation). The energetic wave is what most people focus on, but the subtlety of the water's return is also deeply compelling.

It is Chen's opinion that a large obstacle to a calm, healthy, present existence is the constant interruption of our natural breathing patterns. A thought or ringing phone or honking car interrupts an out-breath and so we stop and begin to inhale. Then we have another thought and stop before exhaling. The result is shallow breathing and deficient flushing of carbon dioxide from our systems, so our cells never have as much pure oxygen as they could. Tai Chi meditation is, among other things, a haven of unimpaired oxygenation.

Whether or not imperfect breath patterns or just plain stress was my problem, my quality of life was greatly improved during my first few months of Tai Chi practice. It was remarkable how developing the ability to be physically introspective changed my world. Aches and pains dissolved with small postural tweaks. If I was stressed out, I did Tai Chi and was calmed. Suddenly I had an internal mechanism with which to deal with external pressures.

On a deeper level, the practice had the effect of connecting disparate elements of my being. My whole life I had been an athletic guy who practiced a sport of the mind. As a boy I had been devoted to my love for chess, and my passion was so unfettered that body and soul were united in the task. Later, as I became alienated from chess, my physical instincts were working in opposition to my mental training. I felt trapped in a cerebral bubble, like a tiger in a cage. Now I was learning how to systematically put those elements of my being back together. In early 1999, Master Chen invited me to begin Push Hands practice. I had no idea that his quiet offer would change my life.

CHAPTER 10

INVESTMENT IN LOSS

When Chen asked me to start attending Push Hands classes, I was of two minds. Up to this point, Tai Chi was a haven. My relationship to it was very personal, and the meditative practice was doing wonders for my life. Stepping into the martial side of the art, I feared, might defeat my purpose. I didn't feel like opposing anybody. I did quite enough of that on the chessboard. But then, with more thought, it seemed like a natural progression: I was able to stay relaxed when doing Tai Chi on my own, and now the challenge would be to maintain and ultimately deepen that relaxation under increasing pressure. Also, from what I had read, the essence of Tai Chi Chuan as a martial art is not to clash with the opponent but to blend with his energy, yield to it, and overcome with softness. This was enigmatic and interesting, and maybe I'd be able to apply it to the rest of my life. Enough said. I was in.

When I walked into my first Push Hands class, it was like entering a different school. I was on the same wooden floor I had been coming to for beginner classes for the past five months, but everything felt heightened. New faces everywhere, a more martial atmosphere. Chen's advanced students filtered throughout the room stretching, working the heavy bag, meditating with mysterious airs. I had no idea what to expect. William Chen walked to the front of the class and we took about six minutes to move through the form, a warm-up that precedes every Push Hands session at the school. Then all the students paired up to begin practice. Master Chen walked over to me, took my arm, and led me to a clear spot on the floor. He raised his wrist, and motioned with his eyes for me to follow. We each stood with our right legs forward, and the backs of our right wrists touching. He asked me to push him.

I pressed into his arm and chest but felt nothing at all. It was bizarre, like hitting a soft void. He was gone and yet he was standing right there in front of me with that same calm expression on his face. I tried again, and this time the lack of resistance seemed to pull me forward. As I adjusted back he barely moved and I went airborne. Interesting. We played a bit more. On a basic level, the idea of Push Hands is to unbalance your opponent, and I tried to apply my old basketball instincts to do so. This guy was sixty-four years old and I was an athlete—shouldn't be a problem. But Chen controlled me without any effort at all. He was inside my skin and I felt like I was doing a moon dance, floating around at his will, without any connection to the ground. At times he felt immovable, like a brick wall, and then suddenly his body would dissolve into cloudlike emptiness. It was astonishing.

After a few minutes, Chen started to show me things. First, he pushed gently on my hip, reminding me that in the Tai Chi form, *sung kwa* or a relaxed hip joint is critical. Then he told me to push into his shoulder, and he slowly laid out the body mechanics of his cloud-like transformation. If I pushed into his right shoulder, his right palm floated up, barely touching my wrist but subtly transferring the focal point away from his shoulder. There was hardly any contact between us, but enough to feel potentially substantial, luring me in. As my push continued, his shoulder dissolved away while the imperceptible resistance from his wrist took its place. The key is that his deflection of my power from his shoulder to his wrist was so subtle that it didn't register in my mind. I gradually overextended because I always felt on the brink of connecting, and before I knew it I was way off balance and stumbling in one direction or another. If I slowed down and tried to notice my point of overextension, then he followed my attempts at correction, sticking to me like glue. When the moment was just right, he'd add to my momentum with a quiet, understated expansion of his arm that defied my understanding of how one generates force—it seemed to emerge from mind more than body—and suddenly I'd be flying away from him. It was amazing how much he could do with so little effort.

From my fledgling moments of Push Hands, I was hooked. It was apparent that the art was infinitely subtle and packed with profound implications, and I knew immediately that the process would be somewhat similar to learning chess. But I had a long way to go.

First things first—I had to begin with an understanding of the art's foundation. The martial philosophy behind Push Hands, in the language of the *Tai Chi Classics,* is "to defeat a thousand pounds with four ounces." Chen's barely perceptible contact between his wrist and my pushing hand was an embodiment of the "four ounces," but there are countless manifestations of this principle inside and outside of Tai Chi—some physical, some psychological. If aggression meets empty space it tends to defeat itself. I guess the perfect image is Lucy snatching the football away time and again as Charlie Brown tries to kick it. Poor Charlie just keeps on flipping himself into the air. The Tai Chi practitioner's body needs to learn how to react quickly and naturally slip away from every conceivable strike. The problem is that we are conditioned to tense up and resist incoming or hostile force, so we have to learn an entirely new physiological response to aggression. Before learning the body mechanics of nonresistance, I had to unlearn my current physical paradigm. Easier said than done.

Try this: Stand up and plant your feet in the ground. Really dig in. Imagine you are on the edge of a cliff. Now ask a friend or sibling or spouse to push into you, and to keep following your attempts at escape with the intention of making your feet move. This can be done very gently. *Both of you should move slowly and smoothly to avoid injury.* My guess is that your physical instinct is to push back, brace yourself, and try to hold your ground.

Now, you have read about the idea of nonresistance. Give it a try. Try to maintain your stance without resisting at all and without moving faster than your opponent. Odds are that unless you are a trained martial artist, this notion feels unnatural. Where are you supposed to go? You might try to retreat into your rear leg, but if your partner follows your retreat, you'll run out of space. At this point, you will resist. If your partner or opponent is stronger than you or has good leverage or momentum built up, you will not be able to stop the incoming power.

Fortunately, we don't learn Push Hands while teetering on the edge of a cliff. It is not a tragedy if we lose our balance. That said, one of the most challenging leaps for Push Hands students is to release the ego enough to allow themselves to be tossed around while they learn how *not to resist.* If a big strong guy comes into a martial arts studio and someone pushes him, he wants to resist and push the guy back to prove that he is a big strong guy. The problem is that he isn't learning anything by doing this. In order to grow, he needs to give up his current mind-set. He needs to lose to win. The bruiser will need to get pushed around by little guys for a while, until he learns how to use more than brawn. William Chen calls this *investment in loss.* Investment in loss is giving yourself to the learning process. In Push Hands it is letting yourself be pushed without reverting back to old habits—training yourself to be soft and receptive when your body doesn't have any idea how to do it and wants to tighten up.

The timing of my life was perfect for this type of process. I was wide open to the idea of getting tossed around—Push Hands class was humility training. Working with Chen's advanced students, I was thrown all over the place. They were too fast for me, and their attacks felt like heat-seeking missiles. When I neutralized one foray, the next came from out of nowhere and I went flying. Chen watched these sessions, and made subtle corrections. Every day, he taught me new Tai Chi principles and refined my body mechanics and technical understanding. I felt like a soft piece of clay being molded into shape.

As the weeks and months passed by, I devoted myself to training and made rapid progress. Working with other beginners, I could quickly find and exploit the tension in their bodies and at times I was able to stay completely relaxed while their attacks slipped by me. While I learned with open pores—no ego in the way—it seemed that many other students were frozen in place, repeating their errors over and over, unable to improve because of a fear of releasing old habits. When Chen made suggestions, they would explain their thinking in an attempt to justify themselves. They were locked up by the need to be correct.

I have long believed that if a student of virtually any discipline could avoid ever repeating the same mistake twice—both technical and psychological—he or she would skyrocket to the top of their field. Of course such a feat is impossible—we are bound to repeat thematic errors, if only because many themes are elusive and difficult to pinpoint. For example, in my chess career I didn't realize I was faltering in transitional moments until many months of study brought the pattern to light. So the aim is to minimize repetition as much as possible, by having an eye for consistent psychological and technical themes of error.

In the last years of my chess career, I was numbed by a building sense of alienation. Pressure messed up my head, and I got stuck, like the guys doing Push Hands who don't learn from their mistakes and practice with a desperate need to win, to be right, to have everything under control. This ultimately cripples growth and makes Tai Chi look like an extension of rush hour in Times Square. In those early Tai Chi years, my mission was to be wide open to every bit of information. I tried my best to learn from each error, whether it was my own or that of a training partner. Each Push Hands class was a revelation, and after a few months I could handle most players who had been studying for a few years.

This was an exciting time. As I internalized Tai Chi's technical foundation, I began to see my chess understanding manifesting itself in the Push Hands game. I was intimate with competition, so offbeat strategic dynamics were in my blood. I would notice structural flaws in someone's posture, just as I might pick apart a chess position, or I'd play with combinations in a manner people were not familiar with. Pattern recognition was a strength of mine as well, and I quickly picked up on people's tells.

As the months turned into years, my training became more and more vigorous and I learned how to dissolve away from attacks while staying rooted to the ground. It is a sublime feeling when your root kicks in, as if you are not standing on the ground but anchored many feet deep into the earth. The key is relaxed hip joints and spring-like body mechanics, so you can easily receive force by coiling it down through your structure. Working on my root, I began to feel like a tree, swaying in the wind up top, but deeply planted down low. In time, I was also able to make my Tai Chi meditation practice manifest in Push Hands play. Techniques that are hidden within the form started to come out of me spontaneously in martial exchanges, and sometimes partners would go flying away from me without my consciously doing much at all. This was trippy, but a natural consequence of systematic training.

I have mentioned how a large part of Tai Chi is releasing tension from your body through the practice of the meditative form. This is effectively a clearing of interference. Now, add in the coordination of breathing with the movements of the form, and what you have is body and mind energizing into action out of stillness. With practice, the stillness is increasingly profound and the transition into motion can be quite explosive—this is where the dynamic pushing or striking power of Tai Chi emerges: the radical change from emptiness into fullness. When delivering force, the feeling inside the body is of the ground connecting to your finger tips, with nothing blocking this communication. Highly skilled Tai Chi practitioners are incredibly fast, fluid, responsive—in a sense, the embodiment of Muhammad Ali's "Float like a butterfly, sting like a bee."

While I was internalizing this information, I was also constantly training with people who were far more advanced. They absolutely manhandled me. There was one man—call him Evan—who was the slightly out-of-control powerhouse of the school. Evan was a six-foot-two, 200-pound second-degree karate black belt, eight-year Aikido student, and eight-year student of Tai Chi. Master Chen only let Evan push with people who could handle his aggression without flipping out, tensing, and getting hurt. But even then, Evan often stirred up confrontations. Once he felt I was ready, Chen started pairing me up with Evan.

Talk about investing in loss! It is one thing to put your ego on hold, but this was brutal. Evan would have me plastered up against a wall, my feet a foot or two off the ground, before I even saw the attack coming. It is in the spirit of Tai Chi training for more advanced students to stop when their partner is off-balance. But Evan had a different style. He liked to put you on the ground. Week after week, I would show up in class and get hammered by Evan. No matter how I tried to neutralize his attacks, I just couldn't do it. He was too fast—how could I dodge what I couldn't see? I knew I should avoid tensing up, but when he came at me my whole body braced for impact. I had no idea how to function from relaxation when a freight train was leveling me fifty times a night. I felt like a punching bag. Basically, I had two options—I could either avoid Evan or get beat up every class.

I spent many months getting smashed around by Evan,

and admittedly it was not easy to invest in loss when I was being pummeled against walls—literally, the plaster was falling off in the corner of the school into which Evan invited me every night. I'd limp home from practice, bruised and wondering what had happened to my peaceful meditative haven. But then a curious thing began to happen. First, as I got used to taking shots from Evan, I stopped fearing the impact. My body built up resistance to getting smashed, learned how to absorb blows, and I knew I could take what he had to offer. Then as I became more relaxed under fire, Evan seemed to slow down in my mind. I noticed myself sensing his attack before it began. I learned how to read his intention, and be out of the way before he pulled the trigger. As I got better and better at neutralizing his attacks, I began to notice and exploit weaknesses in his game, and sometimes I found myself peacefully watching his hands come toward me in slow motion.

There came a moment when the tables clearly turned for me and Evan. My training had gotten very intense, I had won a couple of middleweight National Championship titles, and was preparing for the World Championships. Evan and I hadn't worked together in a while because he started avoiding me as I improved. But this evening Master Chen paired us up on the mats. Evan came at me like a bull, and I instinctively avoided his onslaught and threw him on the floor. He got up, came back at me, and I tossed him again. I was shocked by how easy it felt. After a few minutes of this Evan said that his foot was bothering him and he called it a night. We shook hands, and he would never work with me again.

Reflecting on our relationship, I don't think there was ever any malice in Evan's actions. Truth be told, I think he is a good guy whose no-nonsense, smashmouth approach to martial arts training presented me with a priceless learning opportunity. It's clear that if in the beginning I had needed to look good to satisfy my ego, then I would have avoided that opportunity and all the pain that accompanied it. For his part, Evan was big and strong, and to an inexperienced martial artist he was terrifying, but his forceful approach held him back from internalizing some of the more subtle elements of the art. Most critically, Evan was unwilling to invest in loss himself. He could have taken my improvement as a chance to raise his game, but instead he opted out.

*　*　*

Thinking back on my competitive life, I realize how defining these themes of *Beginner's Mind* and *Investment in Loss* have been. Periodically, I have had to take apart my game and go through a rough patch. In all disciplines, there are times when a performer is ready for action, and times when he or she is soft, in flux, broken-down or in a period of growth. Learners in this phase are inevitably vulnerable. It is important to have perspective on this and allow yourself protected periods for cultivation. A gifted boxer with a fabulous right and no left will get beat up while he tries to learn the jab. Or take the talented high school basketball player learning how to play point guard at the college level. He may have been able to dominate schoolyards in his past, but now he has to learn to see the whole court, share the ball, bring the best out of his teammates. If a young athlete is expected to perform brilliantly in his first games within this new system, he will surely disappoint. He needs time to internalize the new skills before he will improve. The same can be said about a chess player adjusting to a new opening repertoire, a martial artist learning a new technique, or a golfer, for example Tiger Woods, taking apart his swing in order to make a long-term improvement.

How can we incorporate these ideas into the real world? In certain competitive arenas—our working lives, for example—there are seldom weeks in which performance does not matter. Similarly, it is not so difficult to have a beginner's mind and to be willing to invest in loss when you are truly a beginner, but it is much harder to maintain that humility and openness to learning when people are watching and expecting you to perform. True enough. This was a huge problem for me in my chess career after the movie came out. Psychologically, I didn't give myself the room to invest in loss.

My response is that it is essential to have a liberating *incremental* approach that allows for times when you are not in a peak performance state. We must take responsibility for ourselves, and not expect the rest of the world to understand what it takes to become the best that we can become. Great ones are willing to get burned time and again as they sharpen their swords in the fire. Consider Michael Jordan. It is common knowledge that Jordan made more last-minute shots to win the game for his team than any other player in the history of the NBA. What is not so well known, is that Jordan also missed more last-minute shots to lose the game for his team than any other player in the history of the game. What made him the greatest was not perfection, but a willingness to put himself on the line as a way of life. Did he suffer all those nights when he sent twenty thousand Bulls fans home heartbroken? Of course. But he was willing to look bad on the road to basketball immortality.

CHAPTER 11

Making Smaller Circles

My search for the essential principles lying at the hearts of and connecting chess, the martial arts, and in a broader sense the learning process, was inspired to a certain extent by Robert Pirsig's *Zen and the Art of Motorcycle Maintenance*. I'll never forget a scene that would guide my approach to learning for years to come. The protagonist of Pirsig's story, a brilliant if eccentric man named Phaedrus, is teaching a rhetoric student who is all jammed up when given the assignment to write a five-hundred-word story about her town. She can't write a word. The town seems so small, so incidental—what could possibly be interesting enough to write about? Phaedrus liberates the girl from her writer's block by changing the assignment. He asks her to write about the front of the opera house outside her classroom on a small street in a small neighborhood of that same dull town. She should begin with the upper-left hand brick. At first the student is incredulous, but then a torrent of creativity unleashes and she can't stop writing. The next day she comes to class with twenty inspired pages.

I believe this little anecdote has the potential to distinguish success from failure in the pursuit of excellence. The theme is depth over breadth. The learning principle is to plunge into the detailed mystery of the micro in order to understand what makes the macro tick. Our obstacle is that we live in an attention-deficit culture. We are bombarded with more and more information on television, radio, cell phones, video games, the Internet. The constant supply of stimulus has the potential to turn us into addicts, always hungering for something new and prefabricated to keep us entertained. When nothing exciting is going on, we might get bored, distracted, separated from the moment. So we look for new entertainment, surf channels, flip through magazines. If caught in these rhythms, we are like tiny current-bound surface fish, floating along a two-dimensional world without any sense for the gorgeous abyss below. When these societally induced tendencies translate into the learning process, they have devastating effect.

* * *

Let's return to the martial arts. I think it is safe to say that many people consciously or unconsciously associate the term *martial art* with legend and film. We think of ninjas passing invisibly through the night, or shrouded heroes running up walls and flying through the air in *Crouching Tiger Hidden Dragon*. We see wild leaping Van Damme kicks and Jackie Chan flips. We watch completely unrealistic choreography, filmed with sophisticated aerial wires and raucous special effects, and some of us come away wanting to do that stuff too. This leads to the most common error in the learning of martial arts: to take on too much at once. Many "Kung Fu" schools fuel this problem by teaching numerous flowery forms, choreographed sets of movement, and students are rated by how many forms they know. Everyone races to learn more and more, but nothing is done deeply. Things look pretty but they are superficial, without a sound body mechanic or principled foundation. Nothing is learned at a high level and what results are form collectors with fancy kicks and twirls that have absolutely no martial value.

I had a different approach. From very early on, I felt that the moving meditation of Tai Chi Chuan has the primary martial purpose of allowing practitioners to refine certain fundamental principles.* Many of them can be explored by standing up, taking a stance, and incrementally refining the simplest of movements—for example pushing your hands six inches through the air. With the practice of this type of simplified motion you can feel the subtlest ripples inside the body. You become aware of all the tension that resides in your feet, legs, back, and shoulders. Then you release the tension, step by step, hour by hour, month by month, and with the fading of tension comes a whole new world of sensation. You learn to direct your awareness inside the body, and soon enough your fingers come alive with tingling, you feel heat surging up your back and through your arms. The Tai Chi system can be seen as a comprehensive laboratory for internalizing good fundamentals, releasing tension, and cultivating energetic awareness.

I practiced the Tai Chi meditative form diligently, many hours a day. At times I repeated segments of the form over and over, honing certain techniques while refining my body mechanics and deepening my sense of relaxation. I focused on

---

*For example: shifting weight by releasing the hip joints; ever-deepening relaxation; the coordination of mind, breath, and body; awareness of internal energies; winding up to deliver a strike; coiling incoming force down into the ground; rooting; emptying one part of the body while energizing another.

small movements, sometimes spending hours moving my hand out a few inches, then releasing it back, energizing outwards, connecting my feet to my fingertips with less and less obstruction. Practicing in this manner, I was able to sharpen my *feeling* for Tai Chi. When through painstaking refinement of a small movement I had the improved *feeling,* I could translate it onto other parts of the form, and suddenly everything would start flowing at a higher level. The key was to recognize that the principles making one simple technique tick were the same fundamentals that fueled the whole expansive system of Tai Chi Chuan.

This method is similar to my early study of chess, where I explored endgame positions of reduced complexity—for example king and pawn against king, only three pieces on the board—in order to touch high-level principles such as the power of empty space, *zugzwang* (where any move of the opponent will destroy his position), tempo, or structural planning. Once I experienced these principles, I could apply them to complex positions because they were in my mental framework. However, if you study complicated chess openings and middlegames right off the bat, it is difficult to think in an abstract axiomatic language because all your energies are preoccupied with not blundering. It would be absurd to try to teach a new figure skater the principle of relaxation on the ice by launching straight into triple axels. She should begin with the fundamentals of gliding along the ice, turning, and skating backwards with deepening relaxation. Then, step by step, more and more complicated maneuvers can be absorbed, while she maintains the sense of ease that was initially experienced within the simplest skill set.

So, in my Tai Chi work I savored the nuance of small morsels. The lone form I studied was William Chen's, and I took it on piece by piece, gradually soaking its principles into my skin. Every day I did this subtle work at home and then tested it in class at night. It was easy to see whether something worked or not, because training with advanced players like Evan usually involved one of us getting smashed into the wall. In these intense sparring sessions, showy moves didn't work. There was no margin for idealized fanciness. Things happened too quickly. It soon became clear that the next step of my growth would involve making my existing repertoire more potent. It was time to take my new *feeling* and put it to action.

*   *   *

When skilled martial artists face off, it is very different from choreographed Hollywood fight scenes. High-level practitioners rarely overextend, and they know how to read incoming attacks. Large fancy movements like cinematic spinning back-kicks usually don't work. They are too telegraphed and take too long to reach the target. A boxing jab is much more effective because it covers little distance, it's quick, and it's fundamentally sound.

A critical challenge for all practical martial artists is to make their diverse techniques take on the efficiency of the jab. When I watched William Chen spar, he was incredibly understated and exuded shocking power. While some are content to call such abilities *chi* and stand in awe, I wanted to understand what was going on. The next phase of my martial growth would involve turning the large into the small. My understanding of this process, in the spirit of my *numbers to leave numbers* method of chess study, is to touch the essence (for example, highly refined and deeply internalized body mechanics or *feeling*) of a technique, and then to incrementally condense the external manifestation of the technique while keeping true to its essence. Over time expansiveness decreases while potency increases. I call this method "Making Smaller Circles."

Let's combine *Pirsig's Brick* with my concept of *Making Smaller Circles* and see how they work. Let's say that I am cultivating a certain martial technique—for a simple example, a classic straight punch. I stand with my left leg forward, my hands up by my head to protect my face. The jab is a short punch coming from the left, forward hand. The straight is the power punch coming from the ground, generating through my left foot, and moving through my left leg, torso, diagonally across and up to the right side of my back, through the shoulder, tricep, and finally delivered by the second and third knuckles of my right hand. First, I practice the motion over and over in slow motion. We have to be able to do something slowly before we can have any hope of doing it correctly with speed. I release my left hip, wind up, and spring the right hand into motion as my left foot and hip joint spin my waist and upper body into action.

Initially I'll have tension in my shoulder or back, but then I'll sooth it away, slowly repeating the movement until the correct body mechanics are in my skin. Over time, I'm not thinking about the path from foot to fist, I'm just feeling the ground connecting to my fingertips, as if my body is a conduit for the electrical impulse of a punch. Then I start speeding things up, winding up and delivering, over and over. Eventually I start using a heavy bag, practicing these body mechanics with increasing power, building resistance in my body so I can deliver more and more force without hurting myself. My coiling gets stronger and sometimes I hit the bag with a surprising pop. A dangerous moment. When hitting something instead of moving through empty space, I might start to get excited and throw my shoulder into the punch. This is a classic error. It breaks my structure and destroys the connection from foot to fingertip—many boxers make this mistake and come away with shoulder injuries. I want to punch without punching. No intention. My teacher William Chen sometimes teaches punching by telling students to pour a cup of tea. It's a beautiful thing. Pouring tea creates the perfect punch, because people's minds don't get in the way.

Okay, so now weeks and months (maybe years) pass with the cultivation of the right straight punch. I know how to wind up properly. When I hit the bag, nothing hurts, there are no breaks in my structure. It feels as if the ground is smashing the bag through my fist, and my body mechanics are smooth and relaxed. I've also built up quite a bit of power from all the work with winding up, coiling, and releasing the body into motion. When throwing my right, I don't think about anything technical anymore, my body just knows the right feeling and does it. No mind. It's in the blood. I've learned how to throw a straight right. But not really.

The thing is, unless they are flustered or caught in an awkward moment, a good fighter is rarely going to get caught with a big ol' long wound-up straight punch. It's just too obvious. This is where *Making Smaller Circles* comes into play. By now the body mechanics of the punch have been condensed in my mind to a *feeling*. I don't need to hear or see any effect—my body knows when it is operating correctly by an internal sense of harmony. A parallel would be a trained singer who, through years of practice, knows what the notes feel like vibrating inside. Then she is giving a concert in a big venue and the sound system is a nightmare. From onstage, she can't hear herself at all—a surprisingly common occurrence. The great performer can deliver a virtuoso performance without hearing a thing, because she knows how the notes should *feel* coming out, even if her primary monitor—her ears—are temporarily unavailable.

So I know what a properly delivered straight right feels like. Now I begin to slowly, incrementally, condense my movements while maintaining that *feeling.* Instead of a big wind-up in the hips, I coil a little less, and then I release the punch. While initially I may have thrown my straight from next to my ear, now I gradually inch my hand out, starting the punch from closer and closer to the target—and I don't lose power! The key is to take small steps, so the body can barely feel the condensing practice. Each little refinement is monitored by the *feeling* of the punch, which I gained from months or years of training with the large, traditional motion. Slowly but surely, my body mechanics get more and more potent. My waist needs little movement to generate speed. My hand can barely move and still deliver a powerful blow. Eventually I can deliver a straight punch that looks nothing like a straight punch. If you've ever watched some of the most explosive hitters in the boxing world, for instance Mike Tyson or Muhammad Ali, you've seen fights where knockouts look completely unrealistic. Sometimes you have to watch in slow motion, over and over, to see any punch at all. They have condensed large circles into very small ones, and made their skills virtually invisible to the untrained eye.

The chessic manifestations of this phenomenon are quite interesting. For example, arguably the most fundamental chess principle is central control. At all levels of play, the competitor who dominates the middle of the chessboard will usually have an advantage because from this placement his or her pieces can influence the entire battle. Curiously, if you study the games of some very strong Grandmasters, they seem to completely disregard this principle. The British star Michael Adams might be the clearest case in point. His pieces are often on the flanks and he appears to casually give opponents central dominance—and yet he wins. The secret behind this style of play is a profound internalization of the principles behind central domination. Michael Adams knows how to control the center without appearing to have anything to do with the center. He has made the circles so small, even Grandmasters cannot see them.

*　*　*

This concept of *Making Smaller Circles* has been a critical component of my learning process in chess and the martial arts. In both fields, players tend to get attached to fancy techniques and fail to recognize that subtle internalization and refinement is much more important than the quantity of what is learned. I think it was this understanding that won me my first Push Hands National Championship in November 2000, after just two years of Tai Chi study. Surely many of my opponents knew more about Tai Chi than I did, but I was very good at what I did know. I had condensed my body mechanics into a potent state, while most of my opponents had large, elegant, and relatively impractical repertoires. The fact is that when there is intense competition, those who succeed have slightly more honed skills than the rest. It is rarely a mysterious technique that drives us to the top, but rather a profound mastery of what may well be a basic skill set. Depth beats breadth any day of the week, because it opens a channel for the intangible, unconscious, creative components of our hidden potential.

CHAPTER 12

USING ADVERSITY

Super-Heavyweight Finals,
Wong Fei Hung All Kung Fu Championships
September 2001

A 230-pound giant glowered and raised his wrist to mine. His heavy sweating face smelled of rage. This guy was an accomplished fighter with a mean streak and lots of friends at the tournament. He wanted to tear me apart. The referee stood frozen, poised to set us loose for round two. I took a deep breath, exhaled, and felt the blood pumping through my body, the ground soft beneath my feet.

In seven weeks I would defend my title as Tai Chi Chuan Push Hands Middleweight U.S. Champion, and at 170 pounds I had entered the super heavyweight division of a regional tournament for the extra training. Maybe it was bad timing for an experiment, but I was curious to see how I could do against men much bigger and stronger than myself.

In the first round I had neutralized the big man's strength, used it against him. Now I had him mad, aggressive, and off balance. The ref gave the signal and my opponent exploded into me, a brutal attack, coming fast from all angles but somehow in slow motion when I relaxed into the moment. In Tai Chi the artist learns

125

to turn aggression back onto itself, but this is easier said than done when the incoming violence is honed by decades of martial training. My shoulder slipped back when his left hand flew forward, his fist filled the empty space, but then his right hand surged toward my stomach. I melted away before the force connected, caught his right elbow, and followed the momentum. Next thing I knew the guy was flying away from me, spinning twice in the air before righting himself eight feet away. He shook his head and came back at me. Only a minute to go and I will have won the finals. He attacked and I slipped aside, sensed I had him off balance, but then his shoulder ripped into me and I heard a crack. My hand felt icy hot. I knew it was broken. The pain jolted me into deeper focus. Time slowed to a near stop. I didn't show him the injury, quietly fought with one arm, fell into rhythm with his attacks. On the video his hands look like bullets, but in the match they felt like clouds, gently rolling toward me, easily dodged, neutralized, pulled into overextension, exploited. No thought, just presence, pure flow . . . like a chess game.

* * *

When I think of this testing moment in my martial arts career, it reminds me of that afternoon in India some years earlier when an earthquake spurred me to revelation. In both cases, distraction was converted into fuel for high performance. In the chess scene, the shaking jolted my mind into clarity and I discovered the critical solution to the position. In the Push Hands moment, my broken hand made time slow down in my mind and I was able to reach the most heightened state of awareness of my life. In the chapter *The Soft Zone*, I mentioned that there are three critical steps in a resilient performer's evolving relationship to chaotic situations. First, we have to learn to be at peace with imperfection. I mentioned the image of a blade of grass bending to hurricane-force winds in contrast to a brittle twig snapping under pressure. Next, in our performance training, we learn to use that imperfection to our advantage—for example thinking to the beat of the music or using a shaking world as a catalyst for insight. The third step of this process, as it pertains to performance psychology, is to learn to create ripples in our consciousness, little jolts to spur us along, so we are constantly inspired whether or not external conditions are inspiring. If it initially took an earthquake or broken hand for me to gain clarity, I want to use that experience as a new baseline for my everyday capabilities. In other words, now that I have seen what real focus is all about, I want to get there all the time—but I don't want to have to break a bone whenever I want my mind to kick in to its full potential. So a deep mastery of performance psychology involves the internal creation of inspiring conditions. I will lay out my methodology for systematically cultivating this ability in Part III. In this chapter, I will take these three steps of high-performance training and illustrate how they are also critical components of the long-term learning process.

* * *

Let's return to that intense scene in which my broken hand inspired a moment of martial clarity. My perception became so heightened that I saw everything in slow motion. My opponent seemed stuck in molasses while I could move at full speed. The experience was very inspiring and ended up being a beacon for my martial arts training for years to come. However, I faced an immediate problem once the adrenaline faded. I was left with a broken hand seven weeks before the National Championships.

I went to the doctor the day after the injury, hoping for some good news, but after X-rays he told me there was no chance I could compete. I had a spiral fracture in the fourth metacarpal. Best-case scenario, he said, my bone would be fully healed in six weeks but my arm would have atrophied substantially because I would be completely immobilized from the elbow down. I would have just a few days for physical therapy, and it was absurd to consider taking tournament-level impact under those conditions. I walked out of his office resolved to compete, and the day after I got my cast on I was back in training.

My first few days working with one hand, I felt a bit vulnerable. I was worried about someone accidentally knocking into my cast and jolting the injury. I held my right hand behind me, and mostly did sensitivity work with training partners I trusted. We moved slowly, standing up, without throws, doing classical Push Hands in which the two players try to feel each other's centers, neutralize attacks, and subtly unbalance the partner. This isn't ego clashing or direct martial work, but an important method of heightening sensitivity to incoming power and intention—something akin to cooperative martial meditation.

It is very important for athletes to do this kind of visualization work, in a form appropriate to their discipline, but often when we are caught up in the intense routine of training and competition, it feels like we have no time for the internal stuff. I know this quite well. Sometimes when I am in the heat of tournament preparation, months will pass with brutal sparring, constant pain, hitting the mats hundreds of times a night while drilling throws, and then I'll realize that I've moved a bit away from what really makes things tick. Then I'll spend a week doing soft, quiet work on timing, perception, reading and controlling my opponent's breath patterns and internal blinks, subtle unbalancing touches that set up the dramatic throws that ultimately steal the spotlight. After these periods of reflection, I'll almost invariably have a leap in ability because my new physical skills are supercharged by becoming integrated into my mental framework.

The importance of undulating between external and internal (or concrete and abstract; technical and intuitive) training applies to all disciplines, and unfortunately the internal tends to be neglected. Most intelligent NFL players, for example, use the off-season to look at their schemes more abstractly, study tapes, break down aerial views of the field, notice offensive and defensive patterns. Then, during the season they sometimes fall into tunnel vision, because the routine of constant pain requires every last bit of reserves. I have heard quite a few NFL quarterbacks who had minor injuries and were forced to sit out a game or two, speak of the injury as a valuable opportunity to concentrate on the mental side of their games. When they return, they play at a higher level. In all athletic disciplines, it is the internal work that makes the physical mat time click, but it is easy to lose touch with this reality in the middle of the grind.

Since I had broken my right hand, I was forced to cultivate my weaker side. I quickly realized that there were certain martial movements that I relied on my strong hand to cover, and now my left had to catch up so it could do everything. Day by day, my left learned new skills, from deflecting attacks to uprooting someone at unusual angles to eating with chopsticks. After a couple weeks of slow work, my fractured right hand was a bit more stable. I was used to protecting it behind me while playing with my left, and I was also comfortable falling and rolling without touching the injury to the floor, so I was able to mix it up a bit more. Then my teacher began pairing me up with slightly more aggressive training partners who were less skilled than me and not necessarily controlled. A couple of these guys really wanted to prove something. I was a big fish at the school and now was their moment to dominate me. They had two hands, I had one, and they intended to exploit the advantage. Clearly, I had to approach these situations with openness to being tossed around. If I wasn't prepared to invest in loss, there would be no way to do this work. That said, it was fascinating to see how my body reacted. My left arm instinctively became like two arms, with my elbow neutralizing my opponent's right hand and my hand controlling his left arm. I had no idea the body could work this way, and after a few days of this training, the notion that I was playing at a disadvantage faded. I felt completely comfortable with one hand against two, so long as I was a bit more skilled than my partner.

This new perspective opened up a whole new vision of martial intercourse. I realized that whenever I could control two of his limbs with one of mine, I could easily use my unoccupied arm for free-pickings. Today, techniques around this idea are a staple in my competitive martial style. If even for a blink of an eye you can control two of the other guy's limbs with one of yours, either with angle or timing or some sort of clinch, then the opponent is in grave danger. The free hand can take him apart. This principle applies to nearly all contact sports: basketball, football, soccer, wrestling, hockey, boxing, you name it. On the chessboard it is also relevant. Any moment that one piece can control, inhibit, or tie down two or more pieces, a potentially critical imbalance is created on the rest of the board. On a deeper level, this principle can be applied psychologically whenever opposing forces clash. Whether speaking of a corporate negotiation, a legal battle, or even war itself, if the opponent is temporarily tied down qualitatively or energetically more than you are expending to tie it down, you have a large advantage. The key is to master the technical skills appropriate for applying this idea to your area of focus.

I was familiar with this competitive principle from my chess days, but it wasn't until I was forced to train one-handed that I began to understand how potently it could be applied to the martial arts. I would never have guessed that I could control two hands with one in a freestyle exchange, but to be honest, after three or four weeks I became so comfortable fending off both my opponent's hands with my left, that the idea of ultimately getting my right hand back felt like an unfair luxury. This injury was becoming a tremendous source of inspiration.

There was also an intriguing physical component of my recovery. I wanted to compete in the Nationals, so bizarre though it may sound I resolved not to atrophy. At this point in my life I was very involved in the subtle internal dynamics of the body through Tai Chi meditation. I had an idea that I might be able to keep my right side strong by intense visualization practice. My method was as follows: I did a daily resistance workout routine on my left side, and after every set I visualized the workout passing to the muscles on the right. My arm was in a cast, so there was no actual motion possible—but I could feel the energy flowing into the unused muscles. I admit it was a shot in the dark, but it worked. My whole body felt strong, and when the doctor finally took off my cast he was stunned. Four days before the Nationals an X-ray showed that my bone was fully healed, and I had hardly atrophied at all. The doctor cleared me to compete. On Wednesday I did my first weight workout on my right side in seven weeks, on Friday I flew to San Diego, and on Saturday, slightly favoring my newly empowered left arm, I won the Nationals.

*   *   *

One thing I have learned as a competitor is that there are clear distinctions between what it takes to be decent, what it takes to be good, what it takes to be great, and what it takes to be among the best. If your goal is to be mediocre, then you have a considerable margin for error. You can get depressed when fired and mope around waiting for someone to call with a new job offer. If you hurt your toe, you can take six weeks watching television and eating potato chips. In line with that mind-set, most people think of injuries as setbacks, something they have to recover from or deal with. From the outside, for fans or spectators, an injured athlete is in purgatory, hovering in an impotent state between competing and sitting on the bench. In my martial arts life, every time I tweak my body, well-intended people like my mother suggest I take a few weeks off training. What they don't realize is that if I were to stop training whenever something hurt, I would spend my whole year on the couch. Almost without exception, I am back on the mats the next day, figuring out how to use my new situation to heighten elements of my game. If I want to be the best, I have to take risks others would avoid, always optimizing the learning potential of the moment and turning adversity to my advantage. That said, there are times when the body needs to heal, but those are ripe opportunities to deepen the mental, technical, internal side of my game.

When aiming for the top, your path requires an engaged, searching mind. You have to make obstacles spur you to creative new angles in the learning process. Let setbacks deepen your resolve. You should always come off an injury or a loss better than when you went down. Another angle on this issue is the unfortunate correlation for some between consistency and monotony. It is all too easy to get caught up in the routines of our lives and to lose creativity in the learning process. Even people who are completely devoted to cultivating a certain discipline often fall into a mental rut, a disengaged lifestyle that implies excellence can be obtained by going through the motions. We lose presence. Then an injury or some other kind of setback throws a wrench into the gears. We are forced to get imaginative.

Ultimately we should learn how to use the lessons from this type of experience without needing to get injured: a basketball player should play lefty for a few months, to even out his game. A soccer player who favors his right leg should not take a right-footed shot for an extended period of time. If dirty opponents inspire a great competitor to raise his game, he should learn to raise his game without relying on the ugly ruses of his opponents (see *Making Sandals*, in Part III). Once we learn how to use adversity to our advantage, we can manufacture the helpful growth opportunity without actual danger or injury. I call this tool *the internal solution*—we can notice external events that trigger helpful growth or performance opportunities, and then internalize the effects of those events without their actually happening. In this way, adversity becomes a tremendous source of creative inspiration.

CHAPTER 13

SLOWING DOWN TIME

As a child I had a fear that I could never be a chess master because I wouldn't be able to fit all the information into my mind. Sometimes after two hours of a chess lesson, my teacher's words seemed to go in one ear and out the other, and I envisioned a brain filled to the brim. Where could I ever put so much more? And if I did manage to cram everything in there, how would I be able to sort through the stuff? Of course this type of childhood fear is a little silly—skilled humans internalize large amounts of data—but I *was* on to something. Once we reach a certain level of expertise at a given discipline and our knowledge is expansive, the critical issue becomes: how is all this stuff navigated and put to use? I believe the answers to this question are the gateway to the most esoteric levels of elite performance.

Thinking back on the chapter *Making Smaller Circles,* it's apparent that I was focusing on the subtle, introspective cultivation of external skills. Now let's turn further inward, and explore what states of heightened perception can be cultivated with proper training. When I broke my hand in that Super-Heavyweight Finals match, time slowed down in my mind—or my perception became so sharpened, so focused on the essential, that I processed necessary information much more quickly than usual. I didn't feel like I was racing, however. Internally, the experience was profoundly calm with a razor's edge—the epitome of what I think quality presence should be all about.

Once my hand healed and the Nationals were over, the question on my mind was: how can I make time slow down without breaking a limb? Everyone has heard stories of women lifting cars off their children or of time seeming to slow down during a car accident or a fall down the stairs. Clearly, there is a survival mechanism that allows human beings to channel their physical and mental capacities to an astonishing degree of intensity in life-or-death moments. But can we do this at will?

When I started thinking about how I could consistently make my perception of time be different from my opponents', I realized that I had to delve into the operating mechanism of intuition. I suspect we have all had the experience of being stumped by something, eventually moving on to something else, and then suddenly knowing the answer to the initial problem. Most of us have also had the experience of meeting someone and having a powerfully good or bad feeling about them, without knowing why. I have found that, even if a few times it has taken years to pan out, these guiding instincts have been on the money. Along the same lines, in my chess days, nearly all of my revelatory moments emerged from the unconscious. My *numbers to leave numbers* approach to chess study was my way of having a working relationship with the unconscious parts of my mind. I would take in vast amounts of technical information that my brain somehow put together into bursts of insight that felt more like music or wind than mathematical combinations. Increasingly, I had the sense that the key to these leaps was interconnectedness—some part of my being was harmonizing all my relevant knowledge, making it gel into one potent eruption, and suddenly the enigmatic was crystal-clear. But what was really happening?

The question of intuition is hotly debated among psychologists, philosophers, and artists, and it has been a source of much research and thought in my life. My grandmother, Stella Waitzkin, a boldly creative Abstract Expressionist painter and sculptor, used to tell me that intuition was the hand of God. Artists often refer to intuition as a muse. In the introduction, I mentioned that one philosophy professor of mine at Columbia University told me, rather proudly, that the very notion of intuition is incoherent—it doesn't exist. In my opinion, intuition is our most valuable compass in this world. It is the bridge between the unconscious and the conscious mind, and it is hugely important to keep in touch with what makes it tick. If we get so caught up in narcissistic academic literalism that we dismiss intuition as nonexistent because we don't fully understand it, or if we blithely consider the unconscious to be a piece of machinery that operates mystically in a realm that we have no connection to, then we lose the rich opportunity to have open communication with the wellspring of our creativity.

For much of this book I have described my vision of the road to mastery—you start with the fundamentals, get a solid foundation fueled by understanding the principles of your discipline, then you expand and refine your repertoire, guided by your individual predispositions, while keeping in touch, however abstractly, with what you feel to be the essential core of the art. What results is a network of deeply internalized, interconnected knowledge that expands from a central, personal locus point. The question of intuition relates to how that network is navigated and used as fuel for creative insight. Let's begin the plunge into this issue with chess serving as a metaphor for all disciplines.

The clearest way to approach this discussion is with the imagery of *chunking* and *carved neural pathways.* Chunking relates to the mind's ability to assimilate large amounts of information into a cluster that is bound together by certain patterns or principles particular to a given discipline. The initial studies on this topic were, conveniently, performed on chess players who were considered to be the clearest example of sophisticated unconscious pattern integration. The Dutch psychologist Adriaan de Groot (1965) and years later the team of William Simon and Herbert Chase (1973) put chess players of varying skill levels in front of chess positions and then asked them to re-create those positions on an adjacent empty board. The psychologists taped and studied the eye patterns and timing of the players while they performed the tasks.

The relevant conclusions were that stronger players had better memories when the positions were taken out of the games of other strong players, because they re-created the positions by taking parts of the board (say five or six pieces) and chunking (merging) them in the mind by their inter-relationships. The stronger the player, the more sophisticated was his or her ability to quickly discover connecting logical patterns between the pieces (attack, defense, tension, pawn chains, etc.) and thus they had better chess memories. On the other hand, when presented with random chess positions, with no logical cohesiveness, the memories of the players seemed to level off. In some cases the weaker players performed more effectively, because they were accustomed to random situations while the stronger players were a bit lost without "logic to the position." So, in a nutshell, chunking relates to the mind's ability to take lots of information, find a harmonizing/logically consistent strain, and put it together into one mental file that can be accessed as if it were a single piece of information.

By "carved neural pathways" I am referring to the process of creating chunks and the navigation system between chunks. I am not making a literal physical description, so much as illustrating the way the brain operates. Let's say that I spend fifteen years studying chess. During these thousands of hours, my mind is effectively cutting paths through the dense jungle of chess. The jungle analogy is a good one. Imagine how time-consuming it would be to use a machete to cut your way through thick foliage. A few miles could take days. Once the path is cleared, however, you could move quickly through the clearing. If you were to make a road and ride a bike or other vehicle, the transportation would get faster still.

When confronted by a new chess position, initially I have to plod through the variations. During this process, I discover organizing principles and new patterns of movement. This new information gets systematized into a network of chunks that I can access with increasing ease as my navigational function improves.

Now, let's turn to the learning of chess and see how these functions really operate. We will start with day one. The first thing I have to do is to internalize how the pieces move. I have to learn their values. I have to learn how to coordinate them with one another. Early on, these steps might seem complex. There is the pawn, the knight, the bishop, the rook, the queen, and the king. Each piece is unique, with its own strengths and weaknesses. Each time I look at a chess piece I have to remember what it is and how it moves. Then I look at the next piece and try to remember how that one moves. There are initially thirty-two pieces on a chessboard. To make a responsible chess decision, I have to look at all those pieces and check for captures, quick attacks, and other obvious possibilities. By the time I get to the third piece, I'm already a bit overwhelmed. By the tenth piece I have a headache, have already forgotten what I discovered about the first nine pieces, and my opponent is bored. At this point I will probably just make a move and blunder.

So let's say that now, instead of launching from the standard starting position, we begin on an empty board with just a king and a pawn against a king. These are relatively simple pieces. I learn how they both move, and then I play around with them for a while until I feel comfortable. Then, over time, I learn about bishops in isolation, then knights, rooks, and queens. Soon enough, the movements and values of the chess pieces are natural to me. I don't have to think about them consciously, but see their potential simultaneously with the figurine itself. Chess pieces stop being hunks of wood or plastic, and begin to take on an energetic dimension. Where the piece currently sits on a chessboard pales in comparison to the countless vectors of potential flying off in the mind. I see how each piece affects those around it. Because the basic movements are natural to me, I can take in more information and have a broader perspective of the board. Now when I look at a chess position, I can see all the pieces at once. The network is coming together.

Next I have to learn the principles of coordinating the pieces. I learn how to place my arsenal most efficiently on the chessboard and I learn to read the road signs that determine how to maximize a given soldier's effectiveness in a particular setting. These road signs are principles. Just as I initially had to think about each chess piece individually, now I have to plod through the principles in my brain to figure out which apply to the current position and how. Over time, that process becomes increasingly natural to me, until I eventually see the pieces and the appropriate principles in a blink. While an intermediate player will learn how a bishop's strength in the middlegame depends on the central pawn structure, a slightly more advanced player will just flash his or her mind across the board and take in the bishop and the critical structural components. The structure and the bishop are one. Neither has any intrinsic value outside of its relation to the other, and they are chunked together in the mind.

This new integration of knowledge has a peculiar effect, because I begin to realize that the initial maxims of piece value are far from ironclad. The pieces gradually lose absolute identity. I learn that rooks and bishops work more efficiently together than rooks and knights, but queens and knights tend to have an edge over queens and bishops. Each piece's power is purely relational, depending upon such variables as pawn structure and surrounding forces. So now when you look at a knight, you see its potential in the context of the bishop a few squares away. Over time each chess principle loses rigidity, and you get better and better at reading the subtle signs of qualitative relativity. Soon enough, learning becomes unlearning. The stronger chess player is often the one who is less attached to a dogmatic interpretation of the principles. This leads to a whole new layer of principles—those that consist of the exceptions to the initial principles. Of course the next step is for those counterintuitive signs to become internalized just as the initial movements of the pieces were. The network of my chess knowledge now involves principles, patterns, and chunks of information, accessed through a whole new set of navigational principles, patterns, and chunks of information, which are soon followed by another set of principles and chunks designed to assist in the interpretation of the last. Learning chess at this level becomes sitting with paradox, being at peace with and navigating the tension of competing truths, letting go of any notion of solidity.

This is where things get interesting. We are at the moment when psychology begins to transcend technique. Everyone at a high level has a huge amount of chess understanding, and much of what separates the great from the very good is deep presence, relaxation of the conscious mind, which allows the unconscious to flow unhindered. This is a nuanced and largely misunderstood state of mind that when refined involves a subtle reintegration of the conscious mind into a free-flowing unconscious process. The idea is to shift the primary role from the conscious to the unconscious without blissing out and losing the precision the conscious can provide.

For a physical analogy, consider your vision. Let's allow the conscious mind to be represented by your area of visual focus, and your unconscious to be your peripheral vision. Chances are you are sitting down reading this book. What you see is the book. Now if you relax your eyes and allow your peripheral vision to take over, your visual awareness will take in much more, you can see things that are well off to the side. Now, the next step is to refocus on the book, while maintaining a peripheral awareness. This is a skill that some martial artists cultivate for situations with multiple opponents or other such unpredictable occasions. In a relaxed enough state of mind, you can zoom in on something in front of you with great precision while maintaining a very sharp awareness of your surroundings. Along these lines, chess players must let the unconscious flow while the conscious leads and follows, sorting out details, putting things in order, making precise mathematical calculations.

Most people would be surprised to discover that if you compare the thought process of a Grandmaster to that of an expert (a much weaker, but quite competent chess player), you will often find that the Grandmaster consciously looks at less, not more. That said, the chunks of information that have been put together in his mind allow him to see much more with much less conscious thought. So he is looking at very little and seeing quite a lot. This is the critical idea.*

Now, think of me, Josh, competing against a less refined martial artist. Let's say I am in the process of instigating a throw that involves six technical steps. My opponent will experience an indecipherable flurry of action, while for me the six external steps of the throw are just the outer rim of a

---

*A technical example of how this might function in chess is for a player to consider a pair of opposing bishops on a semi-open chessboard. There is a huge amount of information which is fundamental to deciphering the dynamics of those two bishops—that is, central pawn structure, surrounding pieces, potential trades, possible transitions to closed or open games or to endgames of varying pawn structures, initiative, king safety, principles of interpreting these principles, principles of interpreting those interpretive principles, and so on. For the Grandmaster the list is very long. For the expert, it is relatively short. But more importantly, the Grandmaster has a much more highly evolved navigational system, so he can sort through his expansive network of bishop-related knowledge in a flash (he sees bishop and immediately processes all related information), while the expert has to labor through a much smaller amount of data with much more effort. The Grandmaster looks at less and sees more, because his unconscious skill set is much more highly evolved.

huge network of chunks. Our realities are very different. I am "seeing" much more than he is seeing.

Consider one of my favorite judo techniques, a variation of a sacrifice throw—or *sutemi-waza.* I am facing my opponent. My left hand holds his right wrist or sleeve and my right hand holds his collar. The technique involves the following steps: 1) I gently push forward with my right hand on his chest, causing a reactive push back. Following the momentum of his push, 2) I simultaneously pull his right arm forward and across his body, slip my left foot in front of his right foot, pull down with my right hand on his lapel, and sit back while spinning a bit to my left. 3) His right foot is blocked so he has to fall forward, which actually feels okay to him because he will apparently land on top of me. As he starts to fall forward, however, my right foot slips between his legs. 4) As he falls on top of me, I pull his right arm in toward me and kick up against his left inner thigh with my right foot, flipping him over. 5) I roll, following his fall, and end up on top of him. 6) In the transition at the end of this technique, I take his head in what is known as a scarf hold, and trap his right arm in a submission lock.

The first time someone has this rather counterintuitive throw done to them, it will all be a blur—one fast vertiginous experience of being flipped onto the floor and landed on. I speak from experience. I first saw the throw when my close friend Ahmed sprung it on me in training a few years ago. Ahmed is a six-foot-two, 200-pound powerhouse whose martial instincts emerge from a very different place than mine. He is a near Olympic-caliber sprinter, a professional dancer and musician, and a lifetime martial artist, which involves an undefeated Muay Thai full-contact kickboxing record (15–0) and tremendous Jeet Kun Do and karate training. I was pretty skilled in Tai Chi Chuan (had recently won bronze in the World Championships), had some judo experience, and at this time, Ahmed and I were both a little over a year into our study of the grappling art Brazilian Jiu Jitsu with the mind-blowing martial artist and teacher John Machado. Because of our different backgrounds, training with Ahmed often led to creative eruptions. When such knowledge gaps exist, much of the battle involves surviving the unexpected and bringing the game into a place where the neural pathways are carved. Other times, it's like running a gauntlet. When the transition from the familiar to the foreign takes place, it feels like the mind is flying downhill over fresh snow and suddenly hits a patch of thick mud. As an obvious rule, it is good to be the one flying downhill while your opponent is in the mud.

Ahmed and I were in the swirl of free-training, moving fast. I was on my feet, then I was head over heels and on my back before my brain knew what to make of the situation. I hadn't been blindsided like this in quite some time. I immediately asked Ahmed to break down the throw for me and soon enough I saw that the blur involved five or six steps, the foundation of which was a Brazilian Jiu Jitsu sweep I had not really understood. I decided that this was a throw I wanted to cultivate at a very high level. I figured that if it could catch me, it would catch other people. So I started practicing. First I worked on each step slowly, over and over, refining my timing and precision. Then I put the whole thing together, repeating the movements hundreds, eventually thousands of times.

Today, this throw is my bread and butter. In time, each step of the technique has expanded in my mind in more and more detail. The slightest variations in the way my opponent responds to my first push will lead to numerous options in the way I will trigger into the throw. My pull on his right wrist will involve twenty or thirty subtle details with which I will vary my action based on his nuanced microresponses. As I sit back on the ground and trip his right foot, my perception of the moment might involve thirty or forty variations.

Recall that initially I experienced the whole throw as a blur, too fast to decipher, and now we are talking about a tiny portion of the throw involving many distinct moments. When it felt like a blur, my conscious mind was trying to make sense of unfamiliar terrain. Now my unconscious navigates a huge network of subtly programmed technical information, and my conscious mind is free to focus on certain essential details that, because of their simplicity, I can see with tremendous precision, as if the blink in my opponent's eyes takes many seconds.

The key to this process is understanding that the conscious mind, for all its magnificence, can only take in and work with a certain limited amount of information in a unit of time—envision that capacity as one page on your computer screen. If it is presented with a large amount of information, then the font will have to be very small in order to fit it all on the page. You will not be able to see the details of the letters. But if that same tool (the conscious mind) is used for a much smaller amount of information in the same amount of time, then we can see every detail of each letter. Now time feels slowed down.

Another way of understanding this difference in perception is with the analogy of a camera.* With practice I am

---

*The brilliant neurologist Oliver Sacks has explored the imagery of shutter speed in an article for *The New Yorker* and in other writings about the different perceptual patterns of his patients with neurological diseases.

making networks of chunks and paving more and more neural pathways, which effectively takes huge piles of data and throws it over to my high-speed processor—the unconscious. Now my conscious mind, focusing on less, *seems* to rev up its shutter speed from, say, four frames per second to 300 or 400 frames per second. The key is to understand that my trained mind is not necessarily working much faster than an untrained mind—it is simply working more effectively, which means that my conscious mind has less to deal with. Experientially, because I am looking at less, there are, within the same unit of time, hundreds of frames in my mind, and maybe only a few for my opponent (whose conscious mind is bogged down with much more data that has not yet been internalized as unconsciously accessible). I can now operate in all those frames that he doesn't even see.

This is why profoundly refined martial artists can sometimes appear mystical to less skilled practitioners—they have trained themselves to perceive and operate within segments of time that are too small to be perceived by untrained minds.

Now, returning to the scene that initially inspired this movement of thought in my life—does this type of trained enhanced perception I've been discussing come from the same place as those wild moments in life when time slows down in the middle of a car crash or, in my case, when my hand shattered in the ring? The answer is yes and no. The similarity is that a life-or-death scenario kicks the human mind into a very narrow area of focus. Time feels slowed down because we instinctively zero in on a tiny amount of critical information that our processor can then break down as if it is in a huge font. The trained version of this state of mind shares that tiny area of conscious focus. The difference is that, in our disciplines of choice, we cultivate this experience by converting all the other surrounding information into unconsciously integrated data instead of ignoring it. There is a reason the human mind rarely goes into that wild place of heightened perception: if an untrained fighter were to focus all his energy on his opponent's breath pattern or blinking eye, he would get punched in the face or thrown on the ground. If whenever I crossed New York's 33rd Street and Sixth Avenue, I zoned in on some random car that wasn't about to hit me, and I saw it passing in slow motion, then there is a good chance that one of these days I'd get hit by another car. In most situations, we need to be aware of what is happening around us, and our processor is built to handle this responsibility. On the other hand, armed with an understanding of how intuition operates, we can train ourselves to have remarkably potent perceptual and physical abilities in our disciplines of focus. The key, of course, is practice.

CHAPTER 14

THE ILLUSION
OF THE MYSTICAL

Early on in my study of the philosophical foundation of Tai Chi, while scouring through a book of old adages called the *Tai Chi Classics,* I came upon a passage that intrigued me. In the 18th century Wang Tsung-yueh described his practice by writing:

> If the opponent's movement is quick,
> then quickly respond;
> if his movement is slow,
> then follow slowly.

Then the 19th century sage Wu Yu-hsiang built on Tsung-yueh's words with a typically abstract Chinese instructional conundrum:

> If the opponent does not move, then I do not move.
> At the opponent's slightest move, I move first.

The first stanza is rather straightforward. It is about listening, being sensitive to the adversary's slightest tremble, and sticking to him. Adherence is at the center of Tai Chi's martial applicability. Basically those four lines are about becoming a shadow. But the last idea stumped me. A shadow is an effect, not a cause. How do you move *before* someone you are following? The precision of my chess days made me uncomfortable accepting this abstraction on faith. What was it all about?

This question was like a Zen koan to me. I spent countless hours thinking about it, trying to wrap my head around the idea and to embody it in Push Hands training. While it's true that many of the old-school Taoist images should not be taken too literally, there is often a large kernel of experiential truth behind descriptions such as this one. I knew from chess that a superior artist could often get into the head of the opponent, mesmerize him with will or strategic mastery, using what I playfully like to call Jedi Mind Tricks. As far as I understood, the keys to these moments were penetrating insight into what makes the other tick and technical virtuosity that makes the discovery and exploitation invisible to the opponent. On the other hand, Chinese martial arts tend to focus more on energy than pattern recognition. My goal was to find a hybrid—energetic awareness, technical fluidity, and keen psychological perception. Chess meets Tai Chi Chuan.

In time, I have come to understand those words, *At the opponent's slightest move, I move first,* as pertaining to intention—reading and ultimately controlling intention. The deepest form of adherence or shadowing involves a switching of roles, where the follower becomes the followed in a relationship in which time seems to twist in a tangle of minds—this is how the great Tai Chi or Aikido artist guides the opponent into a black hole, or appears to psychically impel the other to throw himself on the ground. But what is really happening? Let's build on the last few chapters and try to break it down.

* * *

My experimentation with intentionality began during my early chess years. I'm a bit embarrassed to admit that as a seven-year-old boy in scholastic chess tournaments, I sometimes lured my young opponents into blundering by 1) making a move that set a trap and then 2) immediately groaning and slapping my head. This over-the-top display would usually inspire a careless moment of overconfidence followed by an eager capture of a poison pawn or some other seductive bait. Not very subtle on my part, I agree. But as with all skills, the most sophisticated techniques tend to have their foundation in the simplest of principles.

As I improved as a chess player and competitor, my opponents and I developed increasingly complex understandings of psychological tells. By the time I was ten or eleven years old, a slap on the head would have been an absurdly transparent display of trickery. But a little change in my breathing pattern might alert a rival that I had just seen something I didn't like.

I don't have much of a natural poker face. I'm an outgoing guy and tend to wear my heart on my sleeve. Instead of trying to change my personality, I learned how to use it to my advantage. While some chess players spend a lot of energy maintaining a stony front, I let opponents read my facial expressions as I moved through thought processes. My goal was to use my natural personality to dictate the tone of the struggle. Just how a poker player might hum a tune to put it in the head of an opponent (thereby "getting in his head"),

I would control the psychology of the game by unmasking myself. If I sat up high in my chair in a natural display of confidence, my opponent might wonder if I was covering something up. Was this reverse psychology? Maybe reverse reverse psychology. Maybe reverse reverse reverse psychology? In addition to the moves I made on the board, I was posing another set of conundrums for an opponent to ponder.

Of course I was not so transparent. Mixed in with my genuine impressions would be misleading furrows of the brow, trickles of fear, or subtle flutters of excitement. Sometimes this type of deception would simply involve the timing of a sip of water or a flicker of my eyes. But not always. Against some rivals, I would be completely straightforward emotionally with no attempt at pretense. This open-book quality might continue from one tournament to the next. Over time, my barely perceptible tells were steadily reliable, and my opponent would trust what he was seeing. Gradually, my mood would become part of his evaluative process—like a leg a martial artist is conditioned to lean on before it is swept away. When the right moment or critical game was at hand, and I was faintly misleading about my current level of confidence, I could provoke an overextension or an overly cautious decision. This was a delicate dance.

At the same time, I was a careful observer of my rivals' rhythms. As I moved into my late teenage years, many of my tournaments were closed, invitational events where ten to fourteen very strong players gathered for two-week marathons. These were psychological wars. Imagine fourteen world-class chess players living together in a small resort above a Bermuda cliff. We ate meals together, took walks on the beach, formed complicated friendships, compared notes about our approaches to the game—and every afternoon at

152

three o'clock, we went to battle. This type of environment was a hotbed of psychological maneuvering.

It was during these years that I began to draw the parallels between people's life tendencies and their chessic dispositions. Great players are all, by definition, very clever about what they show over the chessboard, but, in life's more mundane moments, even the most cunning chess psychologists can reveal certain essential nuances of character. If, over dinner, a Grandmaster tastes something bitter and faintly wrinkles his nose, there might be an inkling of a tell lurking. Impatience while standing on line at the buffet might betray a problem sitting with tension. It's amazing how much you can learn about someone when they get caught in the rain! Some will run with their hands over their heads, others will smile and take a deep breath while enjoying the wind. What does this say about one's relationship to discomfort? The reaction to surprise? The need for control?

By the time I moved into the competitive martial arts, I was very much in tune with my tells, and was quite good at manipulating opponents' impressions of my state of mind. I had also reached a fairly high level of reading psychological wrinkles. It was during these years that I began to cultivate methods of systematically controlling my opponents' intention.

In chess, a huge amount of psychological observation and manipulation might ultimately manifest as a subtle hitch in an opponent's thought process. In physical disciplines like the martial arts, getting into the opponent's head has an immediate and often violent effect that is much more visible to the observing eye. Envision the following scene:

I'm competing against an experienced Push Hands opponent who has fifty pounds on me. He's a good athlete, fast, strong, aggressive. The idea is to stay on your feet and within the ring. In this matchup I'm not going to win with force. It's the mental side of the game that will be critical. The match begins with our right wrists crossed. I apply light pressure on his wrist, and he pushes back. The mood is set. As the play begins we circle one another. I probe him with feints, and each time he comes back at me with a counter attack. We go into the clinch, both of us having our right arms wrapped underneath the opponent's left armpit, both with our right legs forward. I pulse twice with my right shoulder and each time he meets my pulse with resistance. I break out of the clinch. I'm backing up. We play a little more, at a distance. A few times I push into his midsection, and he confidently holds his ground. Then I create an opening, allowing him to close distance and pull me back into the clinch. On the entry I pulse again with my right shoulder, this time very subtly, and immediately trigger into a throw where I empty out my right side and torque him into the hole. He hits the ground hard and is confused. What happened?

This is an overstated example of mental programming. What I did here is observe and provoke a pattern of action/reaction in my opponent. He was much bigger than me, so probably entered the matchup wanting to impose his power. I began by barely pressing against his wrist in the starting position. Here he could have just neutralized my pressure, let it go, but instead he held his ground, pushed back. I have engaged his ego. He is already set up. Next I went into the clinch with the big guy and pushed twice without any ambition to move him. I just wanted to more deeply inspire our rhythm of dance. He's big, I'm small. When I push, he pushes back. If you think about what this means, in that second in which he is responding to my shoulder probe with counterforce, I am supporting some of his weight. I'm becoming one of his legs. When I backed out of the clinch that first time, he felt very good—he's gaining ground, I'm unhappy—so he thinks. I continue to inspire his push-back mentality for a few more moments and then I return to the clinch. This time, my shoulder pulse is very subtle. He does not have to make a decision to push back, it just happens reflexively, but now immediately after my pulse, and actually just before his response begins, I trigger into a throw that is entirely based on his approaching, programmed reaction. I empty out my right side, which has the effect of removing the leg he is just starting to lean on, and I add to his sliver of momentum with a condensed, potent technique. He hits the floor in a blur. Whenever these types of moments happen in the martial arts, it feels a little magical. He experiences standing and then falling into a black hole because our final exchange was all very subtle and perhaps invisible to his conscious mind.

In actual martial play, these types of exchanges are much more refined. Imagine the condensing process of *Making Smaller Circles* applied to the observation and programming side of this interaction. What can really happen is that our wrists meet and I apply the tiniest amount of pressure conceivable. My opponent holds his ground without his conscious mind even realizing that he has responded. He is already set up to be thrown with a one-two combination because his reaction to the *one* is already predictable. I will move before his *two.* Taking this one step further, if my first movement is condensed enough, it will hardly manifest physically at all. My two appears to be a one. *At the opponent's slightest move, I move first.*

* * *

Consider one of the more interesting and psychologically subtle card tricks performed by highly evolved illusionists. A magician is onstage and asks an audience member to join him. When the volunteer (a genuinely unplanted middle-aged man who seems to be enjoying the show) approaches, the performer holds his attention for a few moments while he handles the cards. Then the illusionist lays the fifty-two cards (a real deck) on a table and asks the man to think about a card. Visualize it. The magician then shuffles the cards, lays the deck on the table, and asks the volunteer to flip the top card. It is the envisioned card. What happened here? Did the magician really read the man's mind and then miraculously separate that card from the other fifty-one? Of course not.

This particular illusion is very much in line with the controlling of intention that a martial artist might employ. The key is the subtle manipulation of the volunteer's conscious and unconscious minds. It all happens before the "magic" begins. As the two men stand before one another, in conversation, the illusionist engages the volunteer. This interaction is dictated by the magician. The volunteer is answering questions, following, trying to look good onstage. In the midst of all this, and in a blur that no one in the audience notices, the illusionist flashes a card. This is the sleight of hand. The critical point is that the volunteer must unconsciously notice the card without the observation registering in his conscious mind. He is engaged in the banter of the illusionist, and then suddenly has a seed planted in his mind. When asked to envision a card, that choice has already been made for him. Manipulating the card throughout the shuffle so it remains at the top of the deck is child's play for a halfway-decent sleight of hand artist. The subtlety of this deception is that if the performer fails to fully engage the man's conscious mind, then the clever volunteer will realize he's being programmed and decide to choose another card— the trick won't work.

* * *

If a pattern of interaction is recognizable to the adversary, then mental conditioning will not be terribly effective. In the Push Hands scene I described above, had my opponent recognized that his ego was being manipulated, he could have thwarted my plan. My feigned unhappiness and backing up made him feel powerful, confident, so he was not on the lookout for being set up. This allowed a series of subtle conditioning exchanges, which finally erupted into a throw. If I had really shoved the guy, he surely would have recognized what I was doing. I had to operate beneath his radar.

This is where *Making Smaller Circles* and *Slowing Down Time* come into play. When working with highly skilled and mentally tough opponents, the psychological game gets increasingly subtle. The battle becomes about reading breath patterns and blinks of the eye, playing in frames the opponent is unaware of, invisible technical manipulation that slowly creates response patterns. If I understand a series of movements more deeply, in more frames, with more detail, then I can manipulate my opponent's intention without him realizing what happened.

Here is an example of how this might be done. Stand up with your feet shoulder-width apart. Put your weight in your left leg. Now, imagine somebody is standing on your left side and pushes into your body and up through your left arm with a lot of force. How are you going to keep your balance? Well, you have to lift up your right leg, go with the momentum, and then replant your right foot a couple feet away and land—as if you jumped sideways—no problem. Now put all your weight in your right leg, again, feet shoulder-width apart. If someone were to push you from your left shoulder, you would have a much bigger problem because your right leg is stuck to the ground. A fundamental principle of maintaining balance while moving fast (for example while neutralizing a martial artist's throw or explosive push) is that your feet should never cross. Now when you go airborne, your left foot has to make the long journey past your right if you are going to have any chance of staying up. You'll be all crossed up and probably crash into the ground. This is a simple idea with huge implications.

Much of the Push Hands game takes place with the two players connected up top. Hands and arms are subtly probing for tension. If I push into an opponent, he will either resist my force or empty out the attacked part of his body, dodge the blow, and let the aggression pass by. In either case, there will be a subtle shift in weight. This is a critical moment. In that blur during which someone switches weight from one foot to another, the receiving leg is momentarily stuck. It cannot move. At a high level, athletes have developed very powerful throws. If someone is slightly off balance or unable to move freely with incoming force, he will not be able to catch up before he is hurtling toward the ground. If I trigger a throw toward someone's right foot at the precise moment that his right foot is settling onto the ground, then my opponent will not be able to correct himself. His footwork will get all twisted up. This idea is far from unique to the martial arts. If a tennis player has someone leaning left and hits the ball just out of reach to the right, the opponent will appear flat footed and paralyzed. If an NFL running back, NBA ball handler, or World Cup soccer player can get the defender to put weight in the wrong place at the wrong time, then he can blow on by and leave the guy tripping over himself. In virtually every competitive physical discipline, if you are a master of reading and manipulating footwork, then you are a force to be reckoned with.

So let's build a game around the simple principle of weight redistribution. There are two intertwined components to this process. The first is condensed technique. The second is enhanced perception. Our goal is to take advantage of the moment our opponent is switching his weight from one foot to another. There are many weaknesses or tells that may be used to approach this goal—breath patterns, physical tension, inferior technical understanding, complacency, emotion, distraction, and an array of other unconscious, predictable habits can all be homed in on or combined for the desired effect. For simplicity's sake, let's focus on the eyes. Specifically the blink.

First of all, most people blink without knowing it, so they probably won't consider it a weakness that may be exploited in competition. Even for top competitors, there is not much of a sense of danger associated with the blink—it happens so quickly, everything feels safe. But it isn't. There is a small change in awareness that accompanies the flash of eyes, and a highly skilled player can train himself to exploit it. This is where the methodology of *Slowing Down Time* comes into play. If, through incremental training as described earlier in the book, your unconscious understanding of your discipline of choice has become sufficiently advanced, and you have learned how to trust your physical and intuitive intelligence to handle the technical components of your moment, then your conscious mind can zoom in on very small amounts of data—in this case, the eyes. Because our minds are so complex, if you give us a small amount of material to work with, and we do it with great intensity, then we can break it down into microscopic detail. If our conscious mind is purely focused on the eyes, they will seem to take a while to blink. We see them beginning to close, closed, starting to open, and then open again. That's all we need.

So let's say I am doing Push Hands with a very skilled opponent. I'm in the zone, feeling his weight, his patterns of movement, his eyes. He has certain tells. Before a blink, maybe his cheek twitches. Maybe a touch of moisture forms around his pupil. Or maybe his eyes close a tiny bit, then reopen, then blink. All this is subtle, but I am tapped in. Both of our right legs are forward and we are moving around the ring. In Push Hands you need to hold your ground to stay in the ring. Sometimes you have to root off the rear leg but you don't want to spend too much time with your weight shifted back since that gives you nowhere to go: there's not much give in your structure. Skilled players have internalized this reality, but their training can be used against them. We are flowing. Then, on his blink, or just before it begins, I pulse into a one-two combination, left, right, into his body. My movements are very small; I don't put much force into them. Very little seems to be happening. But my right puts him into his back leg, just barely taking the weight off his front leg. When I release the pressure from my right hand, in the middle of his blink, when his presence is slightly altered, his body instinctively settles back toward his forward leg. In that instant, I trigger into a throw which combines the fact that he is moving forward, providing momentum, and for a microsecond anchoring his forward leg to the floor. If I am good, all this can happen before he has finished blinking. He goes flying onto the ground and comes up confused.

Time and again I have used this type of strategy in competition, and afterward opponents have come over to me and implied that I did something mystical. They were standing and then on the ground, and they didn't feel or see anything occur in-between. Of course there is nothing mystical happening, just the interplay of some interesting psychological, technical, and learning principles. I read his intention to blink and then controlled his intention by determining when he would unconsciously place his weight into his forward leg. If I did this well, my movements—the one-two combination—should barely have been visible. They served the lone purpose of manipulating weight distribution. I should point out that the specific example of using a blink is just one of many options, and it can be neutralized.

When preparing for the 2004 World Championships, my main training partner was my dear friend Daniel Caulfield. Dan is a phenomenal martial artist who placed second in the world in his weight division. He's a fierce competitor, deeply perceptive, with a philosopher's soul that gives his martial style a unique resonance. During our training for the Worlds, Dan and I squared off on the mat every night with the intensity of tournament opponents. It was strange going to war with each other after so many years of friendship. We knew each other's games intimately— there were no technical secrets—so our battles were largely of the mind. In the final three months of preparation, we made the risky agreement to each be responsible for his own safety, which liberated us to play as we would in the championships. There was no holding back. If one of us was slightly off, he got annihilated and had to stew in his juices until the next session. If one of us detected a tell or weakness in the other, he went after it relentlessly until a defensive adjustment was made. We weren't just competing in the ring, we were honing our abilities to read and mask the subtlest signs on the fly.

Dan is a brilliant guy with tremendously explosive power and razor-sharp technique. He knew even my tiniest habits. Every exhalation was dangerous. If my presence diminished for a fraction of a second, I was on the floor. The air felt electric during these sessions. We taped our training and every week I broke down the video. Depending on the day, one or both of us seemed to be operating in a different dimension. Time felt slowed down or sped up. A couple of times when Dan was really on, I blinked and by the time my eyes were open, I was in midair, flying out of the ring. This was my secret! No one had ever turned it on me before. An adjustment was called for, and I got into the habit of taking a tiny step back or pulsing into Dan on my blinks, creating a little space so he couldn't fire in on me. A few times when I was really flowing, I used Dan's awareness of my eye patterns against him, blinking to pull him into an overextension. He quickly caught on to my ruse and our psychology continued to evolve. If both players are aware of a tell, then it will be neutralized, made ineffective, and others will have to be unearthed and exploited. The game goes on.

This type of psychological warfare is at the center of nearly all high-level competitive disciplines—and I mean *competitive* in the loosest sense imaginable. For example, the car salesman and potential buyer are *opponents*. When two highly trained minds square off, in any field, the players are in a fight to enter each other's heads. These exchanges feel like epic tennis rallies in which the tilt of battle sways back and forth as one player picks up on a faint tell that may or may not exist long enough to be exploited, and the other has to feel the danger, and swat the rival out of his mind before it is too late.

While refined mental competitors can have extended dialogues of this nature, in my observation most people are relatively unaware of their psychological subtleties. This makes for easy pickings for the astute rival. So beware when squaring off with a well-versed negotiator, salesman, or lawyer! Understand that the battle stretches well beyond the traditional arena. When one player is more aware of these issues than the other, conditioning is quite simple. Quarterbacks flick their eyes and send safeties flying all over the football field. Real estate moguls furrow their brows, act impatient, check their watches to lull buyers into nervous offers. A chess player observes a rhythm, then sits, lets his clock tick even though a decision has already been reached, then finally makes his move just as the opponent predictably gets up to go to the bathroom. What now? Take a minute, go to the bathroom, come back. Control the pace of the game. Awareness of these dynamics can make you hard to manipulate, and can allow you to turn the tables on even the savviest of conditioners.

To master these psychological battles, it is essential to understand their technical foundation. Contrary to the ego-enforcing descriptions of some "kung fu masters," there is nothing mystical about controlling intention or entering the mind of the opponent. These are skills to be cultivated like any other, and the last few chapters have been my attempt to lay out the road map to their internalization.

PART III

BRINGING IT
ALL TOGETHER

CHAPTER 15

THE POWER OF PRESENCE

In October 2005, I spent two weeks in the Amazon jungle. My father had to go to Brazil to research gold mining operations for his book *The Dream Merchant,* and there was no way I was going to let my pop disappear into the jungle without me. My buddy Dan took the trip with us because he'd always dreamed of the Amazon. We spent much of the trip 250 kilometers south of Manaus, in an area called Tupana, where the outer reaches of the TransAmazonian Highway, the only connection to civilization, dwindle from a pitted two-lane road into a dirt path, with the forest canopy closing in from all sides until the trees are overhead and engulf what remains of the clearing. Every ten or twenty miles, tiny villages exist virtually untouched by the modern world. In this remote part of Brazil, there is a deep respect for the thin line between life and death. There are no layers of protection such as the ones most of us are used to. No grocery stores, no hospitals, no ambulances or policemen to buffer a bad moment. There is the sense among Amazonians that the jungle sits poised to devour the unwary. No one walks into the forest alone. Most people carry weapons. The danger is too great.

While we lived in the rainforest, a man named Manuel acted as our guide. Manuel is a native Amazonian, born in Tupana, about fifty years old, powerfully built with shining brown eyes and the jungle in his blood. He led us through the dense foliage, quietly pointing out medicinal trees, animal tracks, insects, monkey vines, the signs of the forest. From time to time he would stop, raise a hand. Minutes passed. We stood silent and listened, the air alive with the sound of animals feeding or moving nearby. Manuel carried a shotgun. His friend Marcelo trailed us with another. Cats were always on the mind.

Throughout the trip, Dan and I asked a lot of questions about the jaguar. Walking through the forest at night, we wanted to be prepared for an encounter. We were given spears, which made us feel better. But over and over Manuel shook his head and explained that if a jaguar really wants you, there will not be much fight. It is rare for someone to speak of seeing a jaguar in the forest. If you see one, it's probably too late. People traveling in groups will, for the most part, be left alone. From time to time, the last person in a procession will be picked off from behind, but cats generally avoid teams. They are stealth hunters. A lone traveler will be moving through the forest, and the cat will be crouched on a limb of an overhanging tree, blending into the forest canopy, listening, waiting. Then the ambush emerges from nowhere, and the cat is on your neck. In Manuel's descriptions of the jaguar, there seemed to be an almost religious respect for its power, cunning, and intensity. But what if I have a machete? How could I not have a chance?

One evening, lying in hammocks above the forest floor, engulfed by deep blackness and the wild symphony of night sounds, Manuel told us what happened to a friend of his a few years before. This man was named José. He was born in the Amazon. He knew the jungle's sounds, its smells, its signs. He knew how to heal every conceivable ailment with saps and boiled barks of trees, roots, leaves. He climbed vines like a monkey, hunted every evening with a blowgun and darts laced with the venom of poisonous frogs. José could operate from sound and smell alone, freezing in the dark forest, listening, then shooting his dart into the dusky woods and hitting his mark for his family's dinner. He was one of the rare ones who ventured into the forest alone. On these evenings, he wore a mask on his head, eyes pointing backward so the cats would not ambush him from behind. His only weapon was his small blowgun and a machete he apparently wielded like a samurai.

One night José was moving through the forest, darkness closing in, on the way home with a small capybara strapped to his back. Suddenly his skin prickled. He stopped, listened, heard the deep rumble of a cat. He smelled the animal, knew it was near. He felt for his blowgun, but it had been a long night hunting and there were no darts left. José was standing next to a giant Sumaumeira tree, which are often used by Amazonians for communicating over long distances in the jungle. Immediately, José took his machete and swung it back and forth in a blur, clanging against the tree's magnificent exposed root and sending a pounding call for help through the darkness. These vibrations can be heard over a mile away. Hopefully his son would be listening.

Then José stood in silence, waiting. He smelled the cat. It was close. A few moments later a large black jaguar, *onza negra,* over two hundred pounds, glided down from a tree twenty feet ahead of him and started moving in. José remembered the glowing yellow eyes, as though a demon were coming for him. He knew if he ran the cat would be on him instantly. He tossed his night's catch forward onto the forest floor, then held his machete and stood his ground, moving his weapon rhythmically, preparing for the fight of his life. The cat walked straight toward him, and then changed course about eight feet away. It started pacing. Back and forth, keeping distance, but never taking its eyes off José. It watched the machete, followed its movements.

At first, the jaguar's pacing felt good. José thought that maybe it was indecisive, considering the dead rodent. The minutes passed. José's arm got tired from swaying. He watched the rippling muscles of the cat's legs, imagined them hurling the beast on top of him. There would be only one chance. When the cat came, he would need to dodge and strike in a blur. He would have to get to the neck or take off a limb and somehow roll away from the razor claws. It would all happen in an instant. But the waiting was eating him up inside. His whole being was on edge, poised for battle, exploding, while the cat paced, languid, easy, yellow eyes glowing, edging closer, now seven feet away, now six feet. After ten minutes the tension was unbearable. José was drenched in sweat, his right arm shook from the weight of the machete. He switched hands, felt the weapon in his left, hoped the cat didn't notice the new awkwardness for a minute or so while he recovered. He felt dreamy, as if the cat were hypnotizing him. Fear overwhelmed him. This man of the jungle was falling apart.

After fifteen minutes, the cat started moving faster. It edged in, coiled, watched the machete move, then turned back to pacing. It looked for openings, felt the timing of the weapon. José was all strung out. His nerves were frayed. The yellow eyes were taking him over. His body shook. José started sobbing. He backed away from the cat, and this was a mistake. The jaguar moved in. Straight in. It showed its teeth, crouched to leap. José had no fight left. He gave himself up and there was a crack through the night. Then shouting. The cat turned. Another crack rang out and then two young men ran through the bush screaming. José's son took aim with his gun, but the cat vanished into the darkness, leaving a father weeping on the jungle floor. Three years later, José still hadn't recovered from this encounter. The villagers say he went mad. His spirit was broken.

When I heard this story, suspended in the Amazonian night, I was struck by how much I related to both the predator and the prey. I used to create chaos on the chessboard until my opponents crumbled from the pressure. I loved the unknown, the questions, and they wanted answers. When there were no answers, I was home and they were terrified. The game was mine. Then my psychology got complicated and the tables were turned. In my early encounters with world-class Grandmasters, I was usually beaten like José. The chess position might be objectively even, but as the tension on the board mounted it felt as though a vise was slowly cinching down on my head, tighter, tighter, until I reached a bursting point and made some small concession like José backing up, a tiny imprecision that changed the character of the game, anything to release the pressure on my brain. Then they were all over me.

Grandmasters know how to make the subtlest cracks decisive. The only thing to do was become immune to the pain, embrace it, until I could work through hours of mind-numbing complexities as if I were taking a lovely walk in the park. The vise, after all, was only in my head. I spent years working on this issue, learning how to *maintain the ten-*

sion—becoming at peace with mounting pressure. Then, as a martial artist, I turned this training to my advantage, making my opponents explode from mental combustion because of my higher threshold for discomfort.

In every discipline, the ability to be clearheaded, present, cool under fire is much of what separates the best from the mediocre. In competition, the dynamic is often painfully transparent. If one player is serenely present while the other is being ripped apart by internal issues, the outcome is already clear. The prey is no longer objective, makes compounding mistakes, and the predator moves in for the kill. While more subtle, this issue is perhaps even more critical in solitary pursuits such as writing, painting, scholarly thinking, or learning. In the absence of continual external reinforcement, we must be our own monitor, and quality of presence is often the best gauge. We cannot expect to touch excellence if "going through the motions" is the norm of our lives. On the other hand, if deep, fluid presence becomes second nature, then life, art, and learning take on a richness that will continually surprise and delight. Those who excel are those who maximize each moment's creative potential—for these masters of living, presence to the day-to-day learning process is akin to that purity of focus others dream of achieving in rare climactic moments when everything is on the line.

The secret is that everything is always on the line. The more present we are at practice, the more present we will be in competition, in the boardroom, at the exam, the operating table, the big stage. If we have any hope of attaining excellence, let alone of showing what we've got under pressure, we have to be prepared by a lifestyle of reinforcement. Presence must be like breathing.

CHAPTER 16

SEARCHING FOR THE ZONE

How can I learn to enter the zone at will, make it a way of life? How can I maintain my focus under pressure, stay serene and principled under fire, overcome distraction? What do I do when my emotions get out of control?

In Part I, I told the story of my chess career predominantly within the framework of the learning process. Now I'd like to briefly reexamine the arc of those years from the perspective of the performance psychologist. Recall that as a young boy, sometimes I became so deeply immersed in a chess position that the world seemed to fall away. Nothing existed but me and my jungle. During these moments my mother says I seemed to become an old man, as if I knew this game from another life, playing for hours with a focus so intense that she thought her hand would burn if she placed it between my eyes and the board. Other days I would be distracted, chew bubble gum, look around and smile at spectators in Washington Square Park. It was hit or miss, and my poor parents and coach had to sit and deal with whichever Josh showed up that day.

In time, when I started playing tournaments, I had to be more consistent and so I started spending more effort on concentration. I sat at the board when I wanted to walk around. When my mood was flippant, I sucked it up and worked harder. I was an intense competitor, and have never been one to give up on a goal. As a funny aside, my ever-precocious sister started amusing herself with this never-quit aspect of my personality when she was three years old by giving me coconuts to open on Bahamian beaches. I'd spend hours smashing away in the sun, refusing to give up until she was drinking and munching away. In my scholastic chess life I was almost always able to put more energy into the struggle than my opponents. If it was a battle of wills, I won.

When I started competing in adult tournaments, my amped-up energy and focus sometimes worked against me. If you recall the chapter *The Soft Zone*, I began having problems with music or other distractions that got stuck in my mind. Initially I tried to push the world away from me, keep everything silent, but this just amplified the noise. A random song, whispering spectators, distant sirens, ticking chess clocks, would take over my brain until chess became almost impossible to play. Then I had the breakthrough to think to the beat of the song, embrace distraction, and find an inner focus that could exist no matter what the external environment. For years I trained myself to deal with bad conditions, use them to my advantage.

It turns out that the next movement of my life would put this training to the test on a much larger scale. When I was fifteen years old, *Searching for Bobby Fischer* was released and my life went Hollywood. Suddenly I was in the media spotlight and the struggles of the chess world were compounded by extra pressures on my shoulders. When I played tournaments, fans were all over me, cameras followed me around, other players seethed with jealousy. If I had been more mature, I might have been able to translate my youthful experiences with music to this larger form of distraction. But I was off-balance and once again resorted to using my will to block everything out. Instead of rolling with the new vibe of my life, I handled the pressures by putting huge amounts of energy into each chess game.

I recall two moments in particular when I became a man possessed. One game was a critical matchup in the U.S. Junior Championship against the gifted Romanian émi-gré, Grandmaster Gabriel Schwartzman. The other was in the U.S. Championship in 1994, when I squared off against my trainer at the time, Grandmaster Gregory Kaidanov. In both games, the stakes were high, both professionally and emotionally. I was all business, and my intensity was a little wild. Both four-hour struggles passed in a blink. Nothing else existed for me. At one point during our matchup, while I was staring lasers at the board, working my way through the position, Schwartzman walked over to my father, who was in the audience, and told him that he had never seen me like this—he said my concentration was so fierce it was scary sitting across from me. Against Kaidanov, I felt like a tiger in a cage, seething with raw energy. I won both those games, and played some of my most inspired chess, but what is interesting is that afterward I was profoundly depleted and in both cases my tournament immediately fell apart. I blew myself out and had nothing left for the rest of the competitions.

In short, I was a mess. I had learned as a boy how to deal with distraction in a given moment, but the larger distrac-tions of my life were overwhelming me. In an isolated situ-ation, I could overcome the issues—I've always been able to bring it for the big game—but the kind of reckless intensity this required sapped me. At a high level the chess world has many big games and in long, grueling tournaments they tend to follow one another, over and over, for days and weeks at a time. I knew how to block out my issues in a sprint, but in marathons I ran out of gas. Consistency became a critical problem. On days that I was inspired, I was unstoppable. But other days I would play bad chess. The time had come for me to learn the science of long-term, healthy, self-sustaining peak performance.

In the fall of 1996 my father read about the sports psychologist Jim Loehr, who ran a performance training center called LGE in Orlando, Florida. LGE (recently renamed the Human Performance Institute) was founded by Loehr, the esteemed sports nutritionist Jack Groppel, and the no-nonsense physical trainer Pat Etcheberry as an environment in which the physical and mental sides of the pursuit of excellence converged. By the time I first went down to LGE in December of '96, it was already becoming a mecca for athletes who wanted to hone their performance skills, professionalize their nutritional patterns, work out sophisticated everyday training routines to optimize growth, and balance public and personal lives. World-class tennis players, golfers, NFL and NBA stars, Olympic athletes, top CEOs, FBI SWAT teams, basically any kind of elite performer could be found on a given day working out in the high-tech gym, meeting with sports psychologists, or chatting with one another about the similarities of their experiences.

I'll never forget my first afternoon in the LGE weight room. I was working with a trainer, having tests done on me to determine my exact level of fitness. I was using muscles I never knew existed, pushing my physical limits far beyond what I would have known was safe or possible—and I loved it. This was my first exposure to physical training at as high a level of professionalism and sophistication as I had been conditioning my mind for so many years. There I was, sprinting on a high-tech stationary bike, sweating up a storm, hooked up to all sorts of monitors, when a guy slapped me on my back. I turned around to see Jim Harbaugh with a big smile on his face. At the time, Jim was the star quarterback for the Indianapolis Colts. Being a huge Jets fan, I had not always rooted for Jim, but I had watched him play for years and admired his fiery competitive spirit. He had an arm like a cannon, was famous for last-minute comebacks, and was simply a fabulous athlete. I was surprised when Jim told me that he was also an avid chess player and had followed my career for a long time. We fell into a conversation about the psychological parallels of top-notch chess competition and quarterbacking in the NFL. I was amazed by how many of the same issues we wrestled with. I think that this conversation in the LGE gym was my first real inkling of how universal the arts of learning and performance really are.

*　*　*

The two intertwined issues I wanted to take on at LGE were consistency as a competitor and my complicated relationship to the baggage that had come with *Searching for Bobby Fischer.* When I first went down to Orlando shortly after my twentieth birthday, I was still a pretty intuitive performer, operating from a natural mix of intensity, digested experience, and drive. As I described above, when things got rocky, my habit was to hit the gas and blow my opponent and myself out of the water with wildly energetic focus. This was clearly less than an ideal approach for the long term.

The main trainer that I worked with at LGE was a deeply insightful sports psychologist named Dave Striegel. Over the years, Dave and I developed a close relationship and frequently spoke on the phone between my trips to Orlando. Although many valuable insights emerged from our dialogues, perhaps the most explosive revelation emerged from an innocent question during our first meeting. I remember it clearly: after a few hours of conversation in which I described my life, my career, my current issues, Dave sat back, scratched his head, and asked me whether or not I believed the quality of a chessic thought process was higher if it was preceded by a period of relaxation. This simple question led to a revolution in my approach to peak performance.

That evening, after a long day of eye-opening sessions with Dave, Jim Loehr, and Jack Groppel, I sat down with my laptop and chess notebooks and spent a few hours looking over my previous year of competitions. During chess tournaments, players notate their games as they go along. The chessboard is seen as a grid, with vertical ranks running a–h from left to right, and the horizontal files running 1–8, up from white's perspective. After each move, a chess player will write down, for example, Bg4 or Qh5, meaning Bishop moves to g4 or Queen moves to h5. Usually notation is kept on a sheet with a carbon copy beneath, which allows public and private records of all chess games to be saved. For a number of years, when notating my games, I had also written down how long I thought on each move. This had the purpose of helping me manage my time usage, but after my first session with Dave, it also led to the discovery of a very interesting pattern. Looking back over my games, I saw that when I had been playing well, I had two- to ten-minute, crisp thinks. When I was off my game, I would sometimes fall into a deep calculation that lasted over twenty minutes and this "long think" often led to an inaccuracy. What is more, if I had a number of long thinks in a row, the quality of my decisions tended to deteriorate.

The next morning, Striegel and Loehr told me about their concept of *Stress and Recovery*. The physiologists at LGE had discovered that in virtually every discipline, one of the most telling features of a dominant performer is the routine use of recovery periods. Players who are able to relax in brief moments of inactivity are almost always the ones who end up coming through when the game is on the line. This is why the eminent tennis players of their day, such as Ivan Lendl and Pete Sampras, had those strangely predictable routines of serenely picking their rackets between points, whether they won or lost the last exchange, while their rivals fumed at a bad call or pumped a fist in excitement. Consider Tiger Woods, strolling to his next shot, with a relaxed focus in his eyes. Remember Michael Jordan sitting on the bench, a towel on his shoulders, letting it all go for a two-minute break before coming back in the game? Jordan was completely serene on the bench even though the Bulls desperately needed him on the court. He had the fastest recovery time of any athlete I've ever seen. Jim Harbaugh told me about the first time he noticed this pattern in himself. He's a passionate guy, and liked to root on his defense when they were on the field. But after his first sessions at LGE he noticed a clear improvement in his play if he sat on the bench, relaxed, and didn't even watch the other team's offensive series. The more he could let things go, the sharper he was in the next drive.

The notion that I didn't have to hold myself in a state of feverish concentration every second of a chess game was a huge liberation. The most immediate change I made was my way of handling chess games when it was not my turn to move. Instead of feeling obligated to stay completely focused on the chess position while my opponent thought, I began to let my mind release some of the tension. I might think about the position in a more abstract way, or I might even walk away from the board and have a drink of water or wash my face. When my opponent made his move, I would return to the board with renewed energy. Immediately I started noticing improvement in my play.

In the coming months, as I became more attuned to the qualitative fluctuations of my thought processes, I found that if a think of mine went over fourteen minutes, it would often become repetitive and imprecise. After noticing this pattern, I learned to monitor the efficiency of my thinking. If it started to falter, I would release everything for a moment, recover, and then come back with a fresh slate. Now when faced with difficult chess positions, I could think for thirty or forty minutes at a very high level, because my concentration was fueled by little breathers.

At LGE, they made a science of the gathering and release of intensity, and found that, regardless of the discipline, the better we are at recovering, the greater potential we have to endure and perform under stress. That realization is a good starting point. But how do we learn to let go? It is much easier to tell someone to relax than to actually do it on the free-throw line in overtime of the NBA playoffs or in the moments before making a career-defining presentation. This is where the mind-body connection comes in.

The physical conditioners at LGE taught me to do cardio-vascular interval training on a stationary bike that had a heart monitor. I would ride a bike keeping my RPMs over

100, at a resistance level that made my heart rate go to 170 beats per minute after ten minutes of exertion. Then I would lower the resistance level of the bike and go easy for a minute—my heart rate would return to 144 or so. Then I would sprint again, at a very high level of resistance, and my heart rate would reach 170 again after a minute. Next I would go easy for another minute before sprinting again, and so on. My body and mind were undulating between hard work and release. The recovery time of my heart got progressively shorter as I continued to train this way. As I got into better condition, it took more work to raise my heart rate, and less time to lower my heart rate during rest: soon my rest intervals were only forty-five seconds and my sprint times longer.

What is fascinating about this method of physical conditioning is that after just a few weeks I noticed a tangible difference in my ability to relax and recover between arduous thought processes in a chess game. At LGE they had discovered that there is a clear physiological connection when it comes to recovery—cardiovascular interval training can have a profound effect on your ability to quickly release tension and recover from mental exhaustion. What is more, physical flushing and mental clarity are very much intertwined. There was more than one occasion that I got up from the board four or five hours into a hugely tense chess game, walked outside the playing hall, and sprinted fifty yards or up six flights of stairs. Then I'd walk back, wash my face, and be completely renewed.

To this day, virtually every element of my physical training revolves around one form or another of stress and recovery. For example, during weight workouts, the LGE guys taught me to precisely monitor how much time I leave between sets, so that my muscles have ample time to recover, but are still pushed to improve their recovery time. When I began this form of interval training, if I was doing 3 sets of 15 repetitions of a bench press, I would leave exactly 45 seconds between sets. If I was doing 3 sets of 12 repetitions with heavier weights, I would need 50 seconds between sets, if my sets were 10 reps I would take 55 seconds, and if I was lifting heavy weights, at 3 sets of 8 reps, I would take one minute between reps. This is a good baseline for an average athlete to work with. In time, with consistent work, rest periods can be incrementally shortened even as muscles grow and are stressed to their larger healthy limits.

Over the years I have gotten better and better at returning from mental and physical exhaustion. While in my chess career the necessity of such intense body work may seem strange, in my martial arts life it is clear as day—the fighter who can recover in the thirty seconds between rounds and in the irregular intervals between matches will have a huge advantage over the guy who is still huffing and puffing, mentally or physically, from the last battle. On a more dynamic level, in Tai Chi Chuan, real martial power springs from the explosion from emptiness to fullness, or from the soft into the hard. So there are countless moments when I will release all tension for a split second in the midst of a martial flurry. Ultimately, with incremental training very much like what I described in the chapter *Making Smaller Circles,* recovery time can become nearly instantaneous. And once the act of recovery is in our blood, we'll be able to access it under the most strained of circumstances, becoming masters of creating tiny havens for renewal, even where observers could not conceive of such a break.

* * *

In your performance training, the first step to mastering the zone is to practice the ebb and flow of stress and recovery. This should involve interval training as I have described above, at whatever level of difficulty is appropriate for the age and physical conditioning of the individual. This training could, of course, take many forms: I have already mentioned biking and resistance work, but let's say you enjoy swimming laps in a pool. Instead of just swimming until you are exhausted and then quitting, push yourself to your healthy limit, then recover for a minute or two, and then push yourself again. Create a rhythm of intervals like the one I described with my biking. With practice, increase the intensity and duration of your sprint time, and gradually condense rest periods—you are on your way! This same pattern can be used with jogging, weight lifting, martial arts training, or playing any sport that involves cardiovascular work.

If you are interested in really improving as a performer, I would suggest incorporating the rhythm of stress and recovery into all aspects of your life. Truth be told, this is what my entire approach to learning is based on—breaking down the artificial barriers between our diverse life experiences so all moments become enriched by a sense of interconnectedness. So, if you are reading a book and lose focus, put the book down, take some deep breaths, and pick it up again with a fresh eye. If you are at work and find yourself running out of mental stamina, take a break, wash your face, and come back renewed. It would be an excellent idea to spend a few minutes a day doing some simple meditation practice in which your mind gathers and releases with the ebb and flow of your breath. This will help connect your physical interval training to the mental arenas. If you enjoy the experience, gradually build up your mental stamina and spend more time at it. When practiced properly, Tai Chi Chuan, Yoga, or many forms of sitting meditation can be excellent vehicles for this work.

As we get better and better at releasing tension and coming back with a full tank of gas in our everyday activities, both physical and mental, we will gain confidence in our abilities to move back and forth between concentration, adrenaline flow, physical exertion (any kind of stress), and relaxation. I can't tell you how liberating it is to know that relaxation is just a blink away from full awareness. Besides adding to your psychological and physical resilience, this opens up some wonderful and surprising new possibilities. For one thing, now that your conscious mind is free to take little breaks, you'll be delighted by the surges of creativity that will emerge out of your unconscious. You'll become more attuned to your intuition and will slowly become more and more true to yourself stylistically. The unconscious mind is a powerful tool, and learning how to relax under pressure is a key first step to tapping into its potential.

Interval work is a critical building block to becoming a consistent long-term performer. If you spend a few months practicing stress and recovery in your everyday life, you'll lay the physiological foundation for becoming a resilient, dependable pressure player. The next step is to create your trigger for the zone.

CHAPTER 17

BUILDING YOUR TRIGGER

One of the biggest roadblocks to releasing the tension during breaks of intense competition or in any other kind of challenging environment is the fear of whether we will be able to get it back. If getting focused is hit or miss, how can we give up our focus once we've finally got it? Conditioning to this insecurity begins young. As children, we might be told to "concentrate" by parents and teachers, and then be reprimanded if we look off into the stars. So the child learns to associate not focusing with being "bad." The result is that we concentrate with everything we've got until we can't withstand the pressure and have a meltdown. While later on in my career, I sometimes blew myself out with intensity during a game, in my early scholastic chess tournaments my dad and I were very good at preserving my energy. Most of my young rivals had coaches who treated tournaments like military camp. Teachers and parents would make kids analyze their games extensively between rounds, trying to wring a chess lesson out of every moment, while I would be outside having a catch with my dad or taking a nap. Maybe it is no accident that I tended to surge at the end of tournaments. My pop is a clever guy.

This tendency of competitors to exhaust themselves between rounds of tournaments is surprisingly widespread and very self-destructive. Whenever I visit scholastic chess events today, I see coaches trying to make themselves feel useful or showing off for parents by teaching students long technical lessons immediately following a two-hour game and an hour before the next round. Let the kid rest! Fueling up is much more important than last-minute cramming—and at a higher level, the ability to recover will be pivotal. In long chess tournaments that may last for over two weeks, one of the most decisive factors is a competitor's ability to sleep at night. Even the strongest Grandmasters need their energy to come through in the homestretch.

In the martial arts world, this theme is also critical. The ability to wait for hours on end without exploding with tension or losing your edge is often what separates the top fighters before they step in the ring. Big tournaments involve a lot of downtime between matches. Some fighters keep themselves in a state of feverish alertness, always poised for action for fear their moment might come and they won't be ready. The more seasoned competitors relax, listen to headphones, and nap. They don't burn through their tanks before stepping on the mats.

This phenomenon is not unique to the fields I have chosen. We don't live within a Hollywood screenplay where the crescendo erupts just when we want it to, and more often than not the climactic moments in our lives will follow many unclimactic, normal, humdrum hours, days, weeks, or years. So how do we step up when our moment suddenly arises?

My answer is to redefine the question. Not only do we have to be good at waiting, we have to love it. Because waiting is not waiting, it is life. Too many of us live without fully engaging our minds, waiting for that moment when our real lives begin. Years pass in boredom, but that is okay because when our true love comes around, or we discover our real calling, we will begin. Of course the sad truth is that if we are not present to the moment, our true love could come and go and we wouldn't even notice. And we will have become someone other than the *you* or *I* who would be able to embrace it. I believe an appreciation for simplicity, the everyday—the ability to dive deeply into the banal and discover life's hidden richness—is where success, let alone happiness, emerges.

* * *

Along these lines, when considering the issue of performance state, it is important to avoid focusing on those rare climactic moments of high-stakes competitive mayhem. If you get into a frenzy anticipating the moment that will decide your destiny, then when it arrives you will be overwrought with excitement and tension. To have success in crunch time, you need to integrate certain healthy patterns into your day-to-day life so that they are completely natural to you when the pressure is on. The real power of incremental growth comes to bear when we truly are like water, steadily carving stone. We just keep on flowing when everything is on the line.

In recent years I have given many talks on performance psychology. At the beginning of an event in Los Angeles a few years ago, I was approached by a top Smith Barney producer, call him Dennis, who said he was having trouble accessing a good performance state and often found himself distracted in important meetings or under deadline. He asked my advice about how to figure out what his "hot button" was. Dennis knew that some professional athletes have routines that consistently put them into a good frame of mind before competition. He just couldn't find the right routine. No matter how hard he tried to discover the perfect song, meditative technique, stretching exercise, or eating pattern, he just couldn't make it work. Ideally, Dennis said he would like to have a song that slipped him into the zone. What should he do?

This is a problem I have seen in many inconsistent performers. They are frustrated and confused trying to find an inspiring catalyst for peak performance, as if the perfect motivational tool is hovering in the cosmos waiting for discovery. My method is to work backward and create the trigger. I asked Dennis when he felt closest to serene focus in his life. He thought for a moment and told me it was when he played catch with his twelve-year-old son, Jack. He fell into a blissful state when tossing a baseball with his boy, and nothing else in the world seemed to exist. They played catch virtually every day and Jack seemed to love it as much as his dad. Perfect.

I have observed that virtually all people have one or two activities that move them in this manner, but they usually dismiss them as "just taking a break." If only they knew how valuable their breaks could be! Let me emphasize that it doesn't matter what your serene activity is. Whether you feel most relaxed and focused while taking a bath, jogging, swimming, listening to classical music, or singing in the shower, any such activity can take the place of Dennis's catch with his son.

The next step was to create a four- or five-step routine. Dennis had already mentioned music, meditation, stretching, and eating. I suggested that an hour before the next time he played catch with his son, Dennis should eat a light snack. We decided on a blended fruit and soy shake that he enjoyed making in his kitchen. Then he would go into a quiet room and do a fifteen-minute breathing exercise that he had learned a few years before. It was a simple meditative technique where he followed his breath. When he noticed his mind wandering, he just released the thought like a cloud gliding by and returned to his breath. For beginners, this meditation may seem frustrating because they notice their minds racing all over the place and feel that they are doing badly; but that is not the case. The return to breath is the key to this form of meditation. There is no doing badly or well, just being with your breath, releasing your thoughts when you notice them, and coming back to breath. I highly recommend such techniques. Not only is the return to breath a glimmer of the zone—a moment of undistracted presence—but the ebb and flow of the experience is another form of stress and recovery training. Finally, if there is nothing in your life that feels serene, meditation is the perfect hobby to help you discover a launching point in your search for a personalized routine.

Dennis has had a light snack and done some breathing exercises. After these twenty-five minutes, the next step would be a ten-minute stretching routine from his high school football days. I asked Dennis what kind of music he listened to. He had eclectic taste, everything from Metallica to Bob Dylan to classical. I told him that I loved Bob Dylan as well. We decided on "Sad-Eyed Lady of the Lowlands," a beautiful, mellow, *long* Dylan song; but really any music would have worked, depending on the individual's preference. After listening to the song, Dennis would get his son, and they would go outside and toss around the baseball as they did every day. I told Dennis to treat the catch like any other catch, just to have fun.

So we created the following routine:

1. Eat a light consistent snack for 10 minutes
2. 15 minutes of meditation
3. 10 minutes of stretching
4. 10 minutes of listening to Bob Dylan
5. Play ball

For about a month, Dennis went through his routine every day before playing catch with his son. Each step of the routine was natural for him, and playing ball was always a joy, so there was no strain to the experience.

The next step in the process is the critical one: after he had fully internalized his routine, I suggested that he do it the morning before going to an important meeting. So Dennis transplanted his routine from a prelude to playing catch with his son to a prelude to work. He did so and came back raving that he found himself in a totally serene state in what was normally a stressful environment. He had no trouble being fully present throughout the meeting.

The point to this system of creating your own trigger is that a physiological connection is formed between the routine and the activity it precedes. Dennis was always present when playing ball with his son, so all we had to do was set up a routine that became linked to that state of mind (clearly it would have been impractical for Dennis to tow Jack around everywhere he went). Once the routine is internalized, it can be used before any activity and a similar state of mind will emerge. Let me emphasize that your personal routine should be determined by your individual tastes. If Dennis had so chosen, he could have done cartwheels, somersaults, screamed into the wind, and then taken a swim before playing catch with his son, and over time those activities would become physiologically connected to the same state of mind. I tend to prefer a routine like Dennis's, because it is relatively portable and seems more conducive to a mellow presence, but to each his own.

I have used routines before competitions for the last ten years of my life. At chess tournaments, I would meditate for an hour while listening to a tape that soothed me, and then I would go to war. When I started competing in the martial arts I already knew how to get into a peak performance state under pressure and had little trouble dealing with less competitively experienced opponents. Then I ran into a new problem.

In November 2000 I traveled to Taiwan to compete in my first Push Hands World Championship. I had never been to an international martial arts tournament and was awed by the chanting fans in the bleachers and the elaborate traditional opening ceremony in which thousands of competitors marched with their countries' flags waving above. More than fifty nations were represented, each with a unique training style. While I watched the other competitors warm up, I was impressed by their athleticism and obvious mastery. The alien feeling of the environment seemed to heighten the threat of my opponents. I was feeling off-balance so I went into my routine, which at that point was a thirty-minute visualization exercise. I came out of it raring to go. It was 9:00 A.M., I was supposed to have one of the first matches, and I was ready to roll. Then the waiting began.

The clock passed 10:00, then 11:00. I didn't speak the

language and no one would tell me when I was scheduled to compete. I had heard that my opponent was a Taiwanese star, but I had no idea what he looked like. I was hungry, but there was no food available at the arena and my teammates and I had been under the impression that all first-round matches would be early in the morning, so we didn't bring snacks—big mistake. I had been informed that contestants would be announced over the loud speaker five minutes before their match began, and if they failed to show up immediately they would lose by forfeit. So I had to spend hours, hungry, ready to go on immediately for fear of leaving to eat a snack and getting thrown out of the tournament.

Finally at noon a break in the action was announced. Lunch boxes were served to all competitors. At 12:15 I was given a greasy platter of pork fried rice and duck. Far from ideal for the moment, but I was starving and had little choice. So I ate. At 12:30 it was announced that I should report immediately to the judges' table. I was informed my match was starting immediately. My opponent was already warmed up, in a sweat, and had clearly known the exact nature of the tournament schedule. I was disconcerted, unprepared, and had a stomach full of greasy food. I got destroyed. It wasn't even close. It was a little bit of consolation to see my opponent dominate the tournament and go on to win two consecutive World Championships, but I hated the fact that I had traveled all the way to Taiwan and had not even given myself a chance to compete. Some serious adjustments were called for.

First of all, the nutritional side of this story is very important. I should not have trusted the posted schedule and should have had something to sustain me throughout the wait, no matter how long it lasted. I had learned from Jack

Groppel at LGE to eat five almonds every forty-five minutes during a long chess game, to stay in a steady state of alertness and strength. In martial arts tournaments, I now tend to snack on Clif Bars, bananas, and protein shakes whenever necessary. Or, if I know I have at least an hour, I might have a bite of chicken or turkey. Only you know your own body, but the key to nutrition in unpredictable environments like Taiwanese martial arts tournaments is to always be prepared for exertion by being nourished, but never to have too full a stomach and thereby dull your senses.

The nutritional lesson is an easy one: I was careless and paid for it. But a much more serious question arose: what good is a thirty- or forty-five-minute routine if you only have minutes or seconds of warning before the big event? In life, after all, things don't always go according to schedule. Ideally we should be able to click into the zone at a moment's notice. This is where my system for condensing the routine comes in.

Let's return to Dennis. Where we left off, his routine was as follows:

1. Eat a light consistent snack for ten minutes
2. 15 minutes of meditation
3. 10 minutes of stretching
4. 10 minutes of listening to Bob Dylan

He had already learned to export this routine from playing catch with his son Jack, and could now go through the four steps before business meetings or any other stressful event and be in a great state of mind throughout. Dennis loved the results and now did his routine before every meeting. He had taken to scheduling important events right after lunch, so he had some time alone to prepare. He felt great, was more productive, and loved the fresh energy with which he was tackling anything he put his mind (and routine) to. That's already pretty good.

The next step of the process is to gradually alter the routine so that it is similar enough so as to have the same physiological effect, but slightly different so as to make the "trigger" both lower-maintenance and more flexible. The key is to make the changes *incrementally,* slowly, so there is more similarity than difference from the last version of the routine. This way the body and mind have the same physiological reaction even if the preparation is slightly shorter.

Dennis started doing his routine every day before work, the only difference being that he would eat a larger breakfast than the light snack, and he would listen to Dylan during his short drive to the office. Steps two and three took place at home, after breakfast, as originally planned. Everything was going beautifully.

Next, for a few days, Dennis meditated for twelve minutes instead of fifteen. He still came out in the same great state of mind. Then he stretched for eight minutes, instead of ten. Same presence. Then he changed the order of the stretch and meditation. No problem. Over time, slowly but surely, Dennis condensed his stretching and meditation routine down to just a few minutes. Then he would listen to Bob Dylan and be ready to roll. If he wasn't hungry, he could do without the snack altogether. His routine had been condensed to around twelve minutes and was more potent than ever. Dennis left it at that because he loved Dylan so much, but the next step would have been to gradually listen to less and less music, until he only had to think about the tune to click into the zone. This process is systematic, straightforward, and rooted in the most stable of all principles: incremental growth.

As for me, the Tai Chi meditative movements became my routine. Every day before training at my dojo, we took about six minutes and "did the form." Then Push Hands class began, and a number of the top students went at it with the same intensity with which we would approach competition. I learned virtually everything I know about Tai Chi from my years of training in that studio on 23rd Street. There is no place more peaceful and energizing for me. So in addition to the stand-alone benefits of Tai Chi meditation, my body and mind learned to connect the form with my peak performance state because I always did the form before training in my most inspiring setting.

But I did not leave it at that. I had learned that martial arts tournaments are, if anything, unpredictable. We don't always have five minutes of peace and quiet before going to battle. After my disconcerting experience in the 2000 World Championships, I spent a number of months shortening the amount of preparation I needed to be primed for the moment. The essence of the Tai Chi meditative movements is the continued gathering and release of body and mind as the practitioner flows through the various martial postures. As I inhale, my mind comes alive, and I visualize energizing from my feet into my fingers. When I exhale, the mind relaxes, the body de-energizes, lets go, winds up, and prepares for the next inflation. In essence, if you ignore the concrete strengths of the various postures, Tai Chi meditation is the practice of ebb and flow, soft and hard, yin and yang, change. So in theory I should be able to condense the practice to its essence.

Incrementally, I started shortening the amount of form I

did before starting my training. I did a little less than the whole form, then ¾ of it, ½, ¼. Over the course of many months, utilizing the incremental approach of small changes, I trained myself to be completely prepared after a deep inhalation and release. I also learned to do the form in my mind without moving at all. The visualization proved almost as powerful as the real thing. This idea is not without precedent—recall the *numbers to leave numbers, form to leave form,* and *Making Smaller Circles* discussions in Part II. At a high level, principles can be internalized to the point that they are barely recognizable even to the most skilled observers.

I now handle the unpredictability of martial arts tournaments with ease. In fact, the more adverse the environment, the better off I feel, because I know my opponents will not deal with the chaos as well as I will. When I arrive in the tournament hall I get a rough sense for when things will begin. Then I do the Tai Chi form a couple of times, so my body is loose and flowing. I relax, eat a little at a time so I am ready on a moment's notice. If they call my name and say I must report immediately, I go through as much or as little of a routine as I have time for, and I'm good to go. No problem. The ideal for any performer is flexibility. If you have optimal conditions, then it is always great to take your time and go through an extended routine. If things are less organized, then be prepared with a flexible state of mind and a condensed routine.

Of course the advantages to such condensing practice extend far beyond the professional or competitive arenas. If you are driving your car, crossing the street, or doing any other mundane activity, and are suddenly confronted by a potentially dangerous situation, if you are trained to perform optimally on a moment's notice, then you may emerge unscathed from some hair-raising situations. But far more critical than these rare climactic explosions, I believe that this type of condensing practice can do wonders to raise our quality of life. Once a simple inhalation can trigger a state of tremendous alertness, our moment-to-moment awareness becomes blissful, like that of someone half-blind who puts on glasses for the first time. We see more as we walk down the street. The everyday becomes exquisitely beautiful. The notion of boredom becomes alien and absurd as we naturally soak in the lovely subtleties of the "banal." All experiences become richly intertwined by our new vision, and then new connections begin to emerge. Rainwater streaming on a city pavement will teach a pianist how to flow. A leaf gliding easily with the wind will teach a controller how to let go. A housecat will teach me how to move. All moments become each moment. This book is about learning and performance, but it is also about my life. Presence has taught me how to live.

CHAPTER 18

MAKING SANDALS

To walk a thorny road, we may cover its every inch with leather or we can make sandals.

Anger. Fear. Desperation. Excitement. Happiness. Despair. Hope. Emotions are part of our lives. We would be fools to deny such a rich element of the human experience. But, when our emotions overwhelm us, we can get sloppy. If fear reduces us to tears, we might not act effectively in a genuinely dangerous situation. If we seethe when someone crosses us, we may make decisions we come to regret. If we get giddy when things are looking up, we will probably make some careless mistakes that turn our good situation upside down.

Competitors have different ways of approaching their emotions in the heat of battle. Many either feel that their natural movements are irrepressible or fail to consider the question altogether. These are not ideal approaches—if we don't think the issue through, chances are we will be controlled by our passions. There are performers who recognize the disruptive potential of emotions and try to turn them off, become cold, detached, steely. For some personalities this might work, although in my opinion denial tends to melt down when the pressure becomes fierce. Then there are those elite performers who use emotion, observing their moment and then channeling everything into a deeper focus that generates a uniquely flavored creativity. This is an interesting, resilient approach based on flexibility and subtle introspective awareness. Instead of being bullied by or denying their unconscious, these players let their internal movements flavor their fires.

Over the years, at various stages of my development, I have found myself all over this spectrum. In time, I have come to believe that this last style, rooted in my notions of *The Soft Zone* and *The Internal Solution,* is a potent launching point for a unique approach to performance. In this chapter, I'll focus on one of the most decisive emotions, one that can make or break a competitor: Anger. As we enter into this discussion, please keep in mind the three steps I described as being critical to resilient, self-sufficient performance. First, we learn to flow with distraction, like that blade of grass bending to the wind. Then we learn to use distraction, inspiring ourselves with what initially would have thrown us off our games. Finally we learn to re-create the inspiring settings internally. We learn to make sandals.

My own experience with anger in competition began with being jerked around by a rival of mine whom I mentioned in Part I of the book. This kid was a hugely talented Russian player who immigrated to the U.S. when we were fifteen years old. Immediately he and I were the top two young players in the country. Boris knew how to push my buttons. He was unrestrained by any notion of competitive etiquette or even by the rules. He would do everything it took to win, and would sometimes do things so far outside the lines of normal chess behavior that I was totally taken aback. Consider the hilarity of this moment. We are in the U.S. Junior Championship, last round, playing for the title. I am four or five minutes into a deep thought process. This is the critical position. The ideas are coming together, I'm approaching a solution, and suddenly Boris kicks me under the table, two or three times, hard. Boris studied karate and I know he liked to kick things, but this was ridiculous.

There were many times that Boris pummeled me under the table during critical moments of our games, but of course not all of his tactics were so over-the-top. He would shake the board, loudly clear his throat in my face five or six times a minute, tap pieces on the table while I tried to think, or confer about the position in Russian with his coach. The standard reaction to such moments is to go tell the arbiter what is happening. The problem is that when this happened Boris would feign innocence, insist in Russian and broken English that he had no idea what I was talking about, and the arbiter would have nothing to go with. Even if Boris was reprimanded, he had succeeded in getting my mind off the position. He was winning the psychological battle.

I found Boris's disregard for sportsmanship infuriating. People like him hurt the game that I loved. I mentioned in Part I that we both traveled to a world championship in India to represent the United States, and several teams lodged formal protests against the American team because he and his coach were blatantly cheating throughout the event. The whole situation made me sick. The problem is that it also made me angry.

Time and again in critical moments of our games, Boris

201

would pull out some dirty trick, and I would get irritated and make an error. To his credit, Boris knew how to get in my head. As a teenager, anger clouded my vision and Boris played me like a drum. After losing a couple of games to him, I realized that righteous indignation would get me nowhere. I decided to block my anger out. When Boris tapped pieces, I took a deep breath. When he talked about the position with his coach, I just played knowing I would have to beat both of them. When Boris shook the board, I ignored him. This might have seemed a good strategy, but the problem with this approach is that Boris didn't have a limit. He was perfectly content to escalate the situation (for example by leg kick combinations) and eventually I would get pissed off and have a meltdown. It took me some time to realize that blocking out my natural emotions was not the solution. I had to learn to use my moment organically. Instead of being thrown off by or denying my irritation, I had to somehow channel it into a profound state of concentration. It wasn't until my martial arts career that I really learned how to do this.

It took work. The first time this issue came up in my competitive martial arts life was in the finals of my first Tai Chi Chuan Push Hands National Championship in November 2000. I had cruised through the tournament thus far and was in the lead in this match until my opponent head-butted me in the nose, which is blatantly illegal. The referee didn't see it and play continued. The rules of this particular tournament were that points were scored when someone was unbalanced and either thrown into the air, on the ground, or out of a large ring. No blows to the neck, head, or groin were allowed. About fifteen seconds later he head-butted me again, harder, and a wild surge of anger flew up through my body and into my eyes. The blood rush to the eyes that comes with a hard blow to the nose is, I believe, where the expression "seeing red" comes from. I saw red and went out of control for about ten seconds. On the video it looks like my methodical style somehow mutated into a bullish madness. I was over-aggressive, off-balance and completely vulnerable— quite literally, I was blinded by rage. I almost lost the Nationals in those moments, but fortunately I returned to my senses and was able to win the match. A weakness of mine was exposed and luckily I didn't have to lose to learn.

This experience was disturbing to me on a number of levels. There is the competitive angle, but for me there was also a much more important idea at stake. My relationship to the martial arts is rooted in nonviolence. I don't get into fights. I don't want to hurt anyone. I believe that our world is destroying itself with a cycle of violence begetting violence, and I don't want to have any part in that cycle. I first got involved with Tai Chi Chuan as a movement away from ego, away from fighting. I was drawn to the experience of harmony and interconnectedness that felt like a counterpoint to the dog-eat-dog chess world. As I got deeper into the martial side of Tai Chi, and later the grappling art Brazilian Jiu Jitsu, this inner harmony would be tested continuously. To some this might seem like a contradiction—why step into a martial arts ring if you don't want to fight? My personal relationship to this question involves continuous internal cultivation. It is easy to speak of nonviolence when I am in a flower garden. The real internal challenge is to maintain that fundamental perspective when confronted by hostility, aggression, and pain. The next step in my growth process would be to stay true to myself under increasingly difficult conditions.

For the year following this incident at the Nationals, I devoted myself to staying principled when sparring with creeps. I sought out dirty players and got better and better at keeping cool when they got out of control. There were a couple of guys in particular who were very useful to me in this training. I'm sure you remember Evan, the big fellow from the *Investment in Loss* chapter, who used to throw me against the wall. He wasn't a bad guy, but he always pushed me to my limit with his aggression. Much of our training took place during this period of time.

There was another fellow I'll call Frank who was much more of the genuine article. He had been a big Push Hands competitor for a number of years and he didn't like to lose. When he was having trouble, he got dirty. He made his own rules. His particular method of choice was to attack the neck. In Push Hands the target area is shoulders to waist. Bare-handed attacks to the neck can be quite dangerous, and it is normal training etiquette not to target the neck at all. But whenever Frank felt threatened or unstable, he would start jabbing fingers at the Adam's apple. I had one or two ugly experiences with Frank doing this when I was a beginner, well before the Nationals head-butt scene. I didn't like his vibe, felt he was out of control, and for the most part avoided training with him.

Now that changed. I had an issue to work on and Frank would be the ideal training partner. The first step I had to make was to recognize that the problem was mine, not Frank's. There will always be creeps in the world, and I had to learn how to deal with them with a cool head. Getting pissed off would get me nowhere in life.

Once I started training with Frank again, I quickly realized that the reason I got angry when he went after my neck was that I was scared. I didn't know how to handle it and thought I would get hurt. He was playing outside of the rules so a natural defense mechanism of mine was anger and righteous indignation. Just like with Boris. So, first things first—I had to learn to deal with neck attacks. There was a period of months that I asked a few trustworthy training partners of mine to target my neck in Push Hands class. I got used to neutralizing these attacks. Then whenever Frank came into the school, I sought him out and we worked together. Whenever he felt me controlling him, he predictably started going after my neck. When this didn't work, he'd expand his target area, sometimes aiming at an eye, knee, or the groin. My goal was to stay cool under increasingly bad conditions.

After a year of this training, I went back to San Diego to defend my title at the Nationals. Predictably enough, in the finals I faced off with the same guy as the year before. The opening phase of the match was similar to our previous meeting. I began by controlling him, neutralizing his aggression, building up a lead. Then he got emotional and started throwing head-butts. My reaction was very different this time. Instead of getting mad, I just rolled with his attacks and threw him out of the ring. His tactics didn't touch me emotionally, and when unclouded, I was simply at a much higher level than him. It was amazing how easy it all felt when I didn't take the bait.

There were two components to this work. One related to my approach to learning, the other to performance. On the learning side, I had to get comfortable dealing with guys playing outside the rules and targeting my neck, eyes, groin, etc. This involved some technical growth, and in order to make those steps I had to recognize the relationship between anger, ego, and fear. I had to develop the habit of taking on my technical weaknesses whenever someone pushed my limits instead of falling back into a self-protective indignant pose. Once that adjustment was made, I was free to learn. If someone got into my head, they were doing me a favor, exposing a weakness. They were giving me a valuable opportunity to expand my threshold for turbulence. Dirty players were my best teachers.

On the performance side, I had made some strides, but still had a long way to go. First of all, I had to keep my head on straight no matter what. But this was only the initial step of the process. The fact of the matter is that we have our natural responses to situations for a reason. Feelings of anger and fear and elation emerge from deep inside of us and I think blocking them out is an artificial habit. In my experience, competitors who make this mistake tend to crumble when pushed far enough.

I recall reading a *New York Times* article about the New York Jets placekicker Doug Brien days before the Jets took on the Pittsburgh Steelers in the 2004 NFL playoffs. Brien talked confidently about going into a meditative place before every kick. He said that he isolated himself from his surroundings, and he claimed that even under huge pressures his mind was "completely empty" before each kick. When I saw this I felt suspicious about his process—the "completely" bothered me—and I called my dad and told him I was worried about our kicker. Sure enough, when the Jets took on the Steelers, everything came down to two critical kicks. The first one Brien kicked short. The second he shanked way left. In an interview right after the game he said that after the first miss all he could think about was getting it long enough. One miss combined with big pressure to jolt

Brien out of his perfect calm: he fixated on his last mistake and was anything but empty-minded. The fact of the matter is that while I love meditation and believe wholeheartedly in training oneself to operate calmly under pressure, there *is* a difference between the practice field and a hostile, freezing-cold stadium filled with screaming fans who want you to fail in the biggest moment of your life. The only way to succeed is to acknowledge reality and funnel it, take the nerves and use them. We must be prepared for imperfection. If we rely on having no nerves, on not being thrown off by a big miss, or on the exact replication of a certain mindset, then when the pressure is high enough, or when the pain is too piercing to ignore, our ideal state will shatter.

The *Soft Zone* approach is much more organic and useful than denial. The next steps of my growth would be to do with anger what I had with distraction years before. Instead of denying my emotional reality under fire, I had to learn how to sit with it, use it, channel it into a heightened state of intensity. Like the earthquake and the broken hand, I had to turn my emotions to my advantage.

* * *

It has been my observation that the greatest performers convert their passions into fuel with tremendous consistency. There are examples in every discipline. For basketball fans, think about the Reggie Miller/Spike Lee saga. Lee is New York's No. 1 Knicks fan. Reggie Miller was the star of the Indiana Pacers from 1987 to 2005. Throughout the 1990s, the Knicks and Pacers repeatedly met in the playoffs and Lee would be sitting in his courtside seat in Madison Square Garden for every home game. Time and again he would heckle Miller until Miller started to respond. At first this looked like a good situation to Knicks fans. Spike was distracting Reggie from the game. Sometimes it seemed that Reggie was paying more attention to Spike than to the Knicks. But then it became apparent that Miller was using Lee as fuel for his fire. Over and over, Reggie would banter with Spike while torching the Knicks with unbelievable shooting. After a while Knicks fans just hoped Spike would shut up. The lesson had been learned—don't piss off Reggie.

Incidentally, young NBA players learned the same lesson during the Michael Jordan era. Jordan was a notorious trash talker on the court. He would goad defenders into dialogue, but the problem was that if you talked back it inspired Jordan to blow you off the court. The only thing to do was to let Jordan talk and play your game. Try to keep some of the beast asleep. Then he would just score his thirty points and move on to the next game. But if you woke the beast, Mike would score fifty and then do it again next time you played him.

A few years ago I was talking with Keith Hernandez about the role of anger in his career. For those who are not big sports fans, Keith was a dominant force with the St. Louis Cardinals and then the New York Mets, playing Major League Baseball from 1974 to 1990. Keith won 11 Gold Glove awards, won the batting title and National League Most Valuable Player Award in 1979, and led the Mets to victory in the historic 1986 World Series against the Boston Red Sox. Hernandez is known as one of the toughest hitters in baseball history.

I asked Keith how he dealt with pitchers throwing at him. A pitcher will sometimes either hit a batter or come very close to hitting a batter with a pitch in order to plant a psychological seed. Getting nailed by a 90-mph fastball is not a pleasant experience, and many serious injuries have come out of this dark gamesmanship. The infamous scenes of hitters charging the mound and clubhouses emptying into terrible brawls are usually the result of a batter feeling that he is being targeted.

If the batter is actually hit, he automatically gets on first base—as if he were walked. This is obviously less than great for a pitcher, but it is a calculated decision, because many batters will get psyched out by being pelted—and they will be scared at the plate for the rest of the game or even for years when facing that pitcher. Knowing that the fastball might be tailing toward your head complicates the hitting experience, and many batters get intimidated. Or they get mad. Either way, if a pitcher feels that he can get in your head by throwing at you, in Keith's words, "You'll be on your butt!"

For Keith, pitchers dug their own graves by targeting him. He explains: "That was always a positive motivational thing for me; if a pitcher knocked me down or hit me on purpose, well by golly you've got your hands full for the rest of the year with me. Particularly the rest of this game." Over the years pitchers learned to stay away from Keith, because they would be rousing a giant by hitting him.

Keith told me a story about Frank Robinson, one of the all-time greatest baseball players, and the only man to be MVP of both the American League and the National League. Robinson began his career in Cincinnati back in 1956. In those days pitchers threw at batters all the time. The Reds were playing a three-game series against St. Louis, and in the first game, Robinson got hit by a pitch and went on to have a phenomenal night. The next day the pitcher hit Robinson again, and he just destroyed the Cardinals throughout the whole series. A week later, the two teams played another series, but before it began Red Schoendienst, the St. Louis manager—and Keith's first manager—called a team meeting and said "The first pitcher who hits Frank Robinson is fined one hundred bucks! Just leave him alone!" Keith loves this story. It represents what a truly dominant competitor should be all about. Guys like Miller, Jordan, Hernandez, and Robinson are so far beyond shakable that opponents, instead of playing mental games, cower for fear of inspiring them.

*   *   *

Returning to my own experience, I have steadily worked on integrating my natural emotions into creative states of inspiration. Of course there were stages to this process. As a teenager I was thrown off by emotion and tried to block it out. Then, in my early twenties, during my initial experiments with Buddhist and Taoist meditation, I worked on letting my emotions pass like a cloud. This was interesting as it opened up a working relationship with my emotional reality very much like how I described working with the unconscious in the chapter *Slowing Down Time*. Instead of being dominated by or denying my passions, I slowly learned how to observe them and feel how they infused my moment with creativity, freshness, or darkness.

Once I had a working relationship with my emotions, I began to take on my psychological reaction to foul play in the martial arts with a bit more subtlety. I believe that at the highest levels, performers and artists must be true to themselves. There can be no denial, no repression of true personality, or else the creation will be false—the performer will be alienated from his or her intuitive voice. I am a passionate guy. The fact of the matter is that I don't particularly like dirty players. Their relationships to competition, to ego, to sport, to art, to violence, to foul play—it all rubs me the wrong way.

The next step in my training would be to channel my gut reaction into intensity. This is not so hard once you get comfortable in that heated-up place. It is more about sweeping away the cobwebs than about learning anything new. We are built to be sharpest when in danger, but protected lives have distanced us from our natural abilities to channel our energies. Instead of running from our emotions or being swept away by their initial gusts, we should learn to sit with them, become at peace with their unique flavors, and ultimately discover deep pools of inspiration. I have found that this is a natural process. Once we build our tolerance for turbulence and are no longer upended by the swells of our emotional life, we can ride them and even pick up speed with their slopes.

For a period following that second National Championship, I worked on myself. First I learned to stay cool when training with dirty players, and then I started to use my passion to my advantage, to use my natural heat. When working with guys who got out of control, I would feel an organic change in my body chemistry. While initially this may have been disorienting, now I used it to sharpen my game, up the intensity, funnel my primal heat into a penetrating focus. I was no longer being governed by self-protectiveness and fear, and so there was no disorienting anger. In time, I discovered that instead of being thrown off by the likes of Frank, I played my best against them.

My next competitive experience with a dirty player was in the 2002 Push Hands World Championship in Taiwan. Early in my first round of the tournament, the Austrian representative, a noticeably unpleasant man, delivered an entirely illegal and quite painful upper cut to my groin. He was a highly skilled martial artist and I was in a lot of pain—but it was astonishing how his antics backfired. I smiled at him, and he cursed at me. I felt no anger, just resolve. As the match continued, he kept on trying to get in my head in every way imaginable. He went for my groin, tried to take out my knee, continued to attack well after the referee had called stoppages. I didn't react except to buckle down. Every dirty move made me just a little steelier, and what was interesting was that the less his rage affected me, the more flustered he got. He became increasingly aggressive. His failure to get in my head consumed him, made him crazy, and as he got more and more heated he lost track of the technical side of the game and I picked apart his overextensions. This guy was used to rattling opponents with foul play, and by being unmoved, I turned his tactics against him. He landed one cheap shot, but I knocked him out of the tournament.

*   *   *

Of course there is an array of emotions beyond anger that can emerge in pressured scenarios. Truly superb competitive psychologists are finely attuned to their diverse moods and to the creative potential born of them. The former World Chess Champion Tigran Petrosian was known by his rivals to have a peculiar way of handling this issue. When he was playing long matches that lasted over the course of weeks or even months, he would begin each day by waking up and sitting quietly in his room for a period of introspection. His goal was to observe his mood down to the finest nuance. Was he feeling nostalgic, energetic, cautious, dreary, impassioned, inspired, confident, insecure? His next step was to build his game plan around his mood. If he was feeling cautious, quiet, not overwhelmingly confident, he tended to choose an opening that took fewer risks and led to a position that harmonized with his disposition. If feeling energized, aggressive, exceedingly confident, he would pick an opening that allowed him to express himself in a more creative vein. There were countless subtle variations of mood and of opening. Instead of imposing an artificial structure on his match strategy, Petrosian tried to be as true to himself as possible on a moment-to-moment basis. He believed that if his mood and the chess position were in synch, he would be most inclined to play with the greatest inspiration.

Garry Kasparov, World Chess Champion for nearly twenty years and perhaps the strongest chess player of all time, had a different approach to his emotions. Kasparov was a fiercely aggressive chess player who thrived on energy and confidence. My father wrote a book called *Mortal Games* about Garry, and during the years surrounding the 1990 Kasparov-Karpov match, we both spent quite a lot of time with him. At one point, after Kasparov had lost a big game and was feeling dark and fragile, my father asked Garry how he would handle his lack of confidence in the next game. Garry responded that he would try to play the chess moves that he would have played if he were feeling confident. He would pretend to feel confident, and hopefully trigger the state. Kasparov was an intimidator over the board. Everyone in the chess world was afraid of Garry and he fed on that reality. If Garry bristled at the chessboard, opponents would wither. So if Garry was feeling bad, but puffed up his chest, made aggressive moves, and appeared to be the manifestation of Confidence itself, then opponents would become unsettled. Step by step, Garry would feed off his own chess moves, off the created position, and off his opponents' building fear, until soon enough the confidence would become real and Garry would be in flow. If you think back to the chapter *Building Your Trigger* and apply it to this description, you'll see that Garry was not pretending. He was not being artificial. Garry was triggering his zone by playing Kasparov chess.

As you can see, there are many different approaches to handling your emotions under fire. Some are better than others, and at the high end perhaps your personality should determine the nuance of your fine-tuning decisions. That said, I highly recommend that you incorporate the principles of *Building Your Trigger* into your process. Once you are no longer swept away by your emotions and can sit with them even when under pressure, you will probably notice that certain states of mind inspire you more than others. For some it may be happiness, for others it may be fear. To each his own. Petrosian was very flexible. Miller, Hernandez, and Robinson worked well with anger. Kasparov and Jordan were intimidators: they inspired themselves by wilting opponents. Once you understand where you lie on this spectrum, the next step is to become self-sufficient by creating your own inspiring conditions. Kasparov triggered his zone by acting confident and then creating the conditions on the chessboard and a dynamic with his opponent in which he played his best. Miller talked with Spike Lee until he got fired up. When Spike wasn't around, Reggie still liked to play the bad guy. In fact he was at his very best in the playoffs on the road, competing in a stadium filled with hostile fans. If the fans weren't hostile, he might goad them into hating him. Reggie thrived as the villain and triggered these conditions whenever he needed a boost.

But how do you play your best when there is no one around to provide motivation? There is no cookie-cutter mold to inspiration. There is, however, a process we can follow to discover our unique path. First, we cultivate *The Soft Zone*, we sit with our emotions, observe them, work with them, learn how to let them float away if they are rocking our boat, and how to use them when they are fueling our creativity. Then we turn our weaknesses into strengths until there is no denial of our natural eruptions and nerves sharpen our game, fear alerts us, anger funnels into focus. Next we discover what emotional states trigger our greatest performances. This is truly a personal question. Some of us will be most creative when ebullient, others when morose. To each his own. Introspect. Then *Make Sandals,* become your own earthquake, Spike Lee, or tailing fastball. Discover what states work best for you and, like Kasparov, build condensed triggers so you can pull from your deepest reservoirs of creative inspiration at will.

CHAPTER 19

BRINGING IT ALL TOGETHER

Learners and performers come in all shapes and sizes. Some people are aggressive, others are cautious. Some of us like questions, others prefer answers. Some bubble with confidence, always hungering for a challenge, while others break into a sweat at the notion of taking on something new. Most of us are a complicated mix of greys. We have areas of stability and others in which we are wobbly. In my experience the greatest of artists and competitors are masters of navigating their own psychologies, playing on their strengths, controlling the tone of battle so that it fits with their personalities. While in this book I have conveyed my vision of a life of learning, it is my hope that you will take these ideas and make them your own. Make them fit with your natural disposition. I have found that in the intricate endeavors of competition, learning, and performance, there is more than one solution to virtually every meaningful problem. We are unique individuals who should put our own flair into everything we do.

The question is: How do we do this? Let's say we have become very good at something, and we are capable of per-

forming reliably under pressure. How do we become exceptional? How do we make that leap from technical virtuosity
to unique creativity? The real art in learning takes place as we
move beyond proficiency, when our work becomes an expression of our essence. This was the challenge at the center of my
preparation for the 2004 Chung Hwa Cup, the World
Championships of Tai Chi Chuan Push Hands. What was it
inside that could take me to the top?

When I think back on the arc of my competitive Tai Chi
life, Taiwan was always the reality check. It was the true
measure of my growth. The skill level in U.S. Push Hands
events, including our championships, doesn't compare to
such competitions in Taiwan, where Push Hands is the
national sport. Mediocrity can be self-nurturing, and frankly,
many U.S. Push Hands players delude themselves about their
level of proficiency. The top Taiwanese fighters train for
many hours a day from childhood, constantly competing in
brutal regional and national tournaments. For the summer
before the biannual Chung Hwa Cup, the elite schools have
training camps where fighters up the intensity of their
preparation, working six or eight hours a day, combining
intense conditioning with technical sharpening. The stakes
are very high for these competitors, and they are well-oiled
machines when they step in the ring. Foreigners traveling to
the Chung Hwa Cup are entering the den of the lion. Win in
Taiwan and then we can talk about greatness.

The first time I traveled to Taiwan, in 2000, I was fresh off
winning my first Push Hands National Championship. In
more ways than one, I had no idea what I was getting
myself into. I described in *Building Your Trigger* how I got
blindsided by the scheduling of the event. I was told my first
match would be early in the morning but I was faced with

hours of waiting. I got increasingly hungry and had nothing to eat. When the lunch break was announced at noon, I devoured a greasy platter and was immediately called to the ring. I got blown out of the water by the guy who went on to win the tournament. While I certainly needed to take on the psychological side of what happened to have any chance to compete under these conditions, the truth of the matter is that it was not the decisive factor. My opponent was much better than me. If I had been perfectly poised, he would have beaten me. I had a lot to learn.

In the two years following my first experience in Taiwan, I really buckled down in my training. I've described much of that work in the early chapters of Part II, but there was also another component to this preparation. Chinese martial arts tend to be very secretive, and Tai Chi Chuan is a particularly enigmatic discipline. If you read the Tai Chi Classics, study the philosophical foundation, practice the moving meditation, you will gain a sense of awareness, feel supple, and possibly be able to generate a lot of speed and power. But it is hard to translate these principles into viable martial application until you test yourself out in the ring and incrementally separate the real from the mythical. Unfortunately, many teachers haven't done this themselves, and they protect their egos and their schools by claiming to have tremendous power—for example, the ability to throw someone without touching them—but they refuse to show anyone. Often, supposedly great martial artists will avoid demonstrating their "power" by offering the explanation: "If you and I were to spar, I might kill you." Whenever I hear this I know that I am listening to a charlatan—true masters have control. On the other hand, some very powerful skills really can be developed and it is true that the greatest secrets are kept for a very select circle. There is always the lingering question—what is really possible and what is hype?

Until I went to Taiwan, I had no idea what to expect. And sure enough, the top competitors were armed with a skill set I had never dreamed of. They were remarkable athletes who had grown up in a culture that cultivated the refinement of Push Hands in the same way that the old Soviet Union had mastered the engineering of great chess players. Following that first tournament, I was armed with direct observation and many hours of video of the toughest Push Hands players in the world. That video footage of the top Taiwanese competitors would prove to be a crucial well of information.

After my first trip to Taiwan, I saw that the greatest practitioners were not mystics, but profoundly dedicated martial artists who had refined certain fundamental skills at a tremendously high level. The subtlety of their unbalancing techniques was sometimes mind-boggling. While an untrained eye might have seen nothing, these players were using incredibly potent combinations designed to provoke the tiniest of leans—and then opponents were on the floor. From 2000 to 2002, I studied these tapes in detail and slowly refined my game. During those years much of my training was with my dear friend Tom Otterness, who is William Chen's senior student and one of the most powerful internal martial artists I have ever known. Tom is a sculptor who spends his days molding clay and who subsequently has hands and arms that feel like a bear's—add over thirty-five years of Tai Chi training and it's no surprise that Tom hits like an avalanche. When Tom and I first started working together, he would smash me all over the ring. I felt like a tennis ball meeting a wall of force, and to make matters worse Tom was also a heat-seeking missile—there was no avoiding his power. I was forced to add subtlety to my neutralizations and to build up my root* so I could survive his onslaughts. Working with Tom night after night gave me the confidence that I could stand in the ring with anyone.

When I went back to the Chung Hwa Cup in late November 2002, I was ready, or so I thought. By now I had won the U.S. Nationals for three straight years. I regularly competed in multiple weight categories, often giving up over a hundred pounds to my opponents and consistently winning heavyweight and super-heavyweight titles. I was a much improved martial artist and I also knew what I was getting myself into. My first match of that 2002 Chung Hwa Cup was against the Austrian representative, who had just won the European Championship a few months before the Worlds. I described in the previous chapter how early in the match he nailed me with an upper cut to the groin. He was a dirty player who counted on getting into his opponents' heads, but a large part of my training the previous couple of years had been focused on handling his ilk. I buckled down and knocked him out of the tournament.

My next match was against the top student of one of the Taiwanese schools. He was slippery, very fast, but he had a bad habit of rooting off his rear leg when pressured. As I mentioned in *The Illusion of the Mystical,* the problem with putting your weight too far back is that when it shifts forward, as it must inevitably, there is an opening—a flash when

---

*As a reminder, by "root" I am referring to the ability to hold one's ground while directing incoming force down, into the floor. You can then channel the force back up from the ground and bounce an opponent away. When a martial artist is described as having a "deep root" the parallel is to a tree—it feels as if his or her body is extended into the earth.

you are vulnerable. I had been working very hard on my throws for the previous two years, and I was able to work him toward the edge of the ring, make him lean on me, and then use his momentum to put him on the ground. His habitual weight distribution served as a tell and I was all over him. I won the match easily.

Now came the semifinals and my opponent was a Taiwanese star. His name was Chen Ze-Cheng and he was the guy I had been most impressed with two years before. In fact, the video footage I had focused on most closely while preparing for this year's tournament was of Chen Ze-Cheng dismantling his opponents. Chen has the physicality of a gazelle. Tall, sinewy, incredibly strong for his weight, and dazzlingly athletic, he puts opponents on the floor with a speed and technical virtuosity that just baffles the mind. He is the son of the top Push Hands teacher in Taiwan, who is also arguably the best trainer in the world, and so in addition to his physical gifts Chen had been receiving the very best instruction since childhood.

When the opening bell rang, I was all charged up. Our wrists met in the middle of the ring and he immediately shot in for a throw, which I crimped. But he kept the pressure on, pummeling in with his hands to get an advantageous grappling position. I felt danger everywhere. I kept on brushing him away from me, staving off throw after throw, but he wouldn't stop coming. His power felt internal, relaxed, molten, and always primed for an explosion. He was all over me, relentless—but he still hadn't scored any points. A little over halfway through the first round I caught him off-balance in the middle of one of his attacks and exploded into a huge push that sent him flying. It looked like Chen was going out of the ring, but he landed with his toes still in, heels hovering over the line, and he did a matrix maneuver, head backwards nearly to the floor while he pushed out with his waist to keep his balance and stay in bounds. Such an athlete! I charged into the attack but just when I arrived he was upright again and somehow rooted. This was a war.

Playing in that ring with Chen I had the feeling that he was in my skin, sucking out my energy. I kept on pushing him away like a bad dream. I would unbalance him a little, weather his storms, but his conditioning was amazing and he kept coming back. With about thirty seconds to go in the round, I started to feel drained. I have come to understand that this is a big part of Chen's strategy—he pressures opponents, nags them. He is looking for openings but really just goading rivals into exhausting themselves by pushing him away. He keeps pummeling in, getting pushed back, and returning with an endless persistence. I felt this happening and decided to stay in the clinch for a minute, let him in, see if he could do anything. I was on the floor before I could blink.

It was a stunning throw. I was up and then I was down, and I didn't know what hit me. I got up shaking my head and came back at him. There wasn't much time left, and I was overaggressive and got taken down again. The second round was more of the same. He pressured me, I staved him off, searched for openings, but for the most part he felt like a martial giant. About a minute into the round, he caught me flat-footed and the next thing I knew I was piling face first into the mats. Man was he fast! Then he just held me off, protecting his lead. I went after him and was in the middle of a wild attack, a desperate attempt to come back when the bell rang and the match was over. We hugged. He had beaten me with grace and true excellence. My neck and shoulder were throbbing in pain. I was wrecked. I had one more match in the tournament—a fight for third place, which I somehow managed to win despite hardly being able to move the right side of my upper body. So I took bronze in the tournament and had two more years to stew in my juices until my next chance. The bar had been set.

After the 2002 World Championships I was a man on a mission. The time had come to take my game to a new level. I had felt up close and personal what the best in the world was all about and I knew it was within reach. This next phase of my learning process would be about building and refining a competitive repertoire that was uniquely my own. Immediately after coming home to New York City, my work began.

The first couple months of training after the Worlds were mostly mental. For one thing, I had to let my body heal. My shoulder was a mess and it needed some time before it could take full-tilt impact. So I studied tapes, broke down the technical repertoires of Chen Ze-Cheng and the other top Taiwanese players. Watching hours of footage frame by frame I picked up on infinitely subtle setups and plays with footwork that really opened my eyes to what I was up against. The difference between numbers 3 and 1 is mountainous. I would have to become a whole other kind of athlete. Step by step.

By mid January I was back on the mats doing soft training that didn't aggravate the injury but kept my body fluid. I worked on some new technical ideas, integrated the movements into my arsenal by doing slow-motion repetitions. By March I could mix it up at full speed without worrying about my shoulder, but I still wasn't playing competitively so much as working on the ideas I described in the chapters

Making Smaller Circles, Slowing Down Time, and *The Illusion of the Mystical.* I was still in the "research and development" stage.

I have talked about style, personal taste, being true to your natural disposition. This theme is critical at all stages of the learning process. If you think about the high-end learning principles that I have discussed in this book, they all spring out of the deep, creative plunge into an initially small pool of information. In the early chapters, I described the importance of a chess player laying a solid foundation by studying positions of reduced complexity (*endgame before opening*). Then we apply the internalized principles to increasingly complex scenarios. In *Making Smaller Circles* we take a single technique or idea and practice it until we feel its essence. Then we gradually condense the movements while maintaining their power, until we are left with an extremely potent and nearly invisible arsenal. In *Slowing Down Time,* we again focus on a select group of techniques and internalize them until the mind perceives them in tremendous detail. After training in this manner, we can see more frames in an equal amount of time, so things feel slowed down. In *The Illusion of the Mystical,* we use our cultivation of the last two principles to control the intention of the opponent—and again, we do this by zooming in on very small details to which others are completely oblivious.

The beautiful thing about this approach to learning is that once we have felt the profound refinement of a skill, no matter how small it may be, we can then use that feeling as a beacon of quality as we expand our focus onto more and more material. Once you know what *good* feels like, you can zero in on it, search it out regardless of the pursuit. On a large scale, this is how I translated my understanding of chess to the martial arts. On a smaller, more focused scale, this is how I trained for the 2004 World Championships.

While this principle of penetrating the macro through the micro is a critical idea in the developmental process, it is also an absolutely pivotal foundation for a great competitor. At the highest levels of any kind of competitive discipline, everyone is great. At this point the decisive factor is rarely who knows more, but who dictates the tone of the battle. For this reason, almost without exception, champions are specialists whose styles emerge from profound awareness of their unique strengths, and who are exceedingly skilled at guiding the battle in that direction.

With this in mind, my training for the 2004 World Championships would have to be built around my core strengths. Sure, I am a good athlete, but frankly there would be many fighters in Taiwan who were more gifted than me physically. Some would be stronger, some would be faster, some would have more endurance. But there would be no other fighter who could keep up with me strategically. To win in the Chung Hwa Cup, I would have to bring water to their fire. I wouldn't be successful making the fights a test of speed and acrobatics. I would have to read opponents and shut them down, confront them with strategies and refinements they couldn't imagine. To have any chance in the ring with him, I would have to dictate the tone of battle and make Chen Ze-Cheng play chess with me.

I had one good thing going for me. As I described in the end of Part II, my main training partner in my preparations for the tournament was my friend Dan Caulfield. Dan is an incredible natural athlete and a lifetime martial artist. Since childhood, a huge part of Dan's life has been devoted to exploring the outer reaches of his physical potential. As a boy growing up in rural New Hampshire, he taught himself to jump from higher and higher surfaces until he could comfortably leap off a thirty-foot roof, land in a roll, and come up running. If you point to a car, if he is in the mood, Dan will jump over it. If you look at a steep cliff or a brick wall, Dan can figure out how to climb it. If you go hiking with Dan, he leaps from boulder to boulder up the mountain like a goat. Add in over fifteen years of Aikido and Tai Chi Chuan training, and you've got yourself a force to be reckoned with.

The lucky thing for me was that Dan is built somewhat like Chen Ze-Cheng, he shares Chen's enormous physical talent, and stylistically they are both predators. While both are technically masterful, they also have the tendency to take big risks, believing in their athleticism to help them recover if put into a bad position. This is what I had to build on. To win in Taiwan, I would have to use Chen's greatness against him.

In the two years before the 2004 Taiwan tournament, Dan and I basically lived on the mats together. Some nights we were drilling techniques, building the power of our throws while the other was just a body, hitting the ground a hundred times before switching roles. In other sessions we were refining footwork, breaking down the precise components of going with momentum when someone has an edge and tries to spin you to the floor or out of the ring. It's amazing how you can land on your feet and balanced if you know how to stay calm and principled, embrace the chaos, while you are spun with a torque that sends sweat hitting walls ten feet away. But more often than not Dan and I were duking it out. Night after night we had brutal sessions, spending hours in the ring, squaring off, clashing, neutralizing attacks, exploding onto weaknesses, hitting the ground, getting back up, and colliding again like rams.

Dan and I continuously pushed each other to improve. We were both working so hard that if one of us stopped learning, he would get killed in the ring. It was during the last four months of our preparation that I came upon my fundamental strategy for the tournament—what chess players call prophylaxis. You see, I believe that Dan, like Chen Ze-Cheng, is a more gifted athlete than me. For all my training, he can do things that boggle my mind. So when working with Dan I developed a game that was based on squelching his talents. In Taiwan I would play in the style of Karpov or Petrosian, the Grandmasters who triggered my existential crisis at the end of my chess career.

In the last months of Taiwan training, instead of trying to blow Dan out of the ring, I tried to shut him down, crimp his game, and use the tiniest overextensions to my advantage. I created an approach we called the Anaconda. I would pressure my opponent, stifle his attacks, slowly inch him out of the ring while cutting off escape paths. If my opponent breathed, I would take space when he exhaled. This was a game that relied on keen presence and sensitivity to my opponent's intention. Every aggressive move in a martial arts confrontation is risky. To attempt a throw, you weaken your structure if only for a flash. I would use that flash. Whenever Dan tried to throw me, I entered the attack, took space, and tried to simultaneously neutralize his aggression and cinch down the pressure.

Week after week, I got better at this. I was creating the anti-Chen Ze-Cheng game. And Dan got better at attacking me. Some nights I would dominate him, repress his every attack, and then explode in my own throws when he got desperate. Other nights he would be electric and destroy me. I remember one night in particular when he felt like a jaguar. He was all over me, above me, behind me, on fire with an animal inspiration. I limped home feeling absolutely bereft, but the next night I came in and locked him down.

For the final three months before Taiwan, I recorded all of Dan's and my training sessions. Then, every night I would go home and study the tapes. This was valuable on a number of mundane levels. Watching yourself on video, you can spot tells or bad habits. You can refine your techniques by breaking down what works and what doesn't. But the primary function the tapes had for me was very different.

Dan and I had both reached such a high level of presence to incoming aggression that our sessions were marked by fewer and fewer points. We knew each other's games, we knew what attacks were coming, we knew how to probe without overextending. Dan had figured out how to play against my right shoulder in a manner that neutralized most of my aggressive impulses, and I could usually take advantage of his attacks to edge him out of the ring. If you took our physical and mental abilities, put them together, and collided them on the mats, we were dead even. We were also performing at peak levels, so few mistakes were being made. We were in a state of dynamic equilibrium. The only times points were scored were in moments of creative inspiration, when one of us did something that transcended our current level of ability. These were the moments I focused on in the videos.

Two or three times in an evening, Dan and I would be in the middle of a wild flurry and suddenly my body would put his body on the ground. Just like that. And two or three times, he would do the same to me. We were playing with such a tight margin, that I couldn't think about a technique and then do it to him. No way it would catch him off-guard. But a few times my instincts would find something that my conscious mind didn't pick up on.

When I went home and watched the video, I studied each of these moments frame by frame to see what happened. Sometimes I would see myself triggering into a throw just as Dan's blink began. Other times, my body would direct a throw off to a creative new angle that caught Dan unawares. Maybe my footwork would fall into rhythm with his in a manner that opened up a tiny gap of momentum to ride, or I might catch him at the beginning of an exhalation. There were many moments like this, each of which I studied until I understood. The next day I would come into training and tell Dan what I discovered. We would then convert what had been creative inspiration into something we understood technically. If my body synched up with his breathing, we broke down how to do this at will. If I caught a blink, we studied the nuances of blinking. Next time we sparred, Dan would be aware of the new weapon I was working with, and so he would create a counter in order to stay in the game. Then I would work against his counter. This way we raised the baseline of our everyday level, and incrementally expanded the horizon of what our creative bursts could attain.

Let's think about this method in the language of chess: If a chess expert were to have his most inspired day he would come up with ideas that would blow his mind and the minds of others at his level. But for the master, these inspired creations would be humdrum. They are the everyday because his knowledge of chess allows him to play this way all the time. While the weaker player might say, "I just had a feel-

ing," the stronger player would shrug and explain the principles behind the inspired move. This is why Grandmasters
can play speed chess games that weaker masters wouldn't
understand in hundreds of hours of study: they have internalized such esoteric patterns and principles that breathtakingly
precise decisions are made intuitively. The technical afterthoughts of a truly great one can appear to be divine inspiration to the lesser artist.

When I think about creativity, it is always in relation to
a foundation. We have our knowledge. It becomes deeply
internalized until we can access it without thinking about it.
Then we have a leap that uses what we know to go one or
two steps further. We make a discovery. Most people stop
here and hope that they will become inspired and reach
that state of "divine insight" again. In my mind, this is a
missed opportunity. Imagine that you are building a
pyramid of knowledge. Every level is constructed of technical information and principles that explain that information
and condense it into chunks (as I explained in the chapter
Slowing Down Time). Once you have internalized enough
information to complete one level of the pyramid, you move
on to the next. Say you are ten or twelve levels in. Then you
have a creative burst like the ones Dan and I had in the ring.
In that moment, it is as if you are seeing something that is
suspended in the sky just above the top of your pyramid.
There is a connection between that discovery and what you
know—or else you wouldn't have discovered it—and you can
find that connection if you try. The next step is to figure out
the technical components of your creation. Figure out what
makes the "magic" tick.

The way this process functioned with Dan and me was
that my body would somehow put him on the ground. The

way I did it was outside both our conceptual schemes, so neither of us really knew what happened. Then I went home and studied the tape. I saw, for example, that my throw triggered from a precise grappling position at the exact moment that Dan's left foot received his weight from his right foot. I didn't do this consciously—my body just did it instinctively. But now we have learned that in that particular position, an opponent is vulnerable when he shifts his weight in that manner. The next step for me is to create techniques that force the switch of weight. And Dan can become more conscious to avoid the trap. We both get better and better at playing around the split second when the weight settles on the ground through the left foot. We have created a body of theory around a fleeting moment of inspiration. Now there are techniques and principles that make this weapon accessible all the time. We have taken our pyramid of knowledge up one level and solidified a higher foundation for new leaps.

After seven or eight weeks of this work, we had internalized a very tight network of martial arts techniques that were all the products of Dan's and my most inspired moments. This became our championship arsenal. What we constructed was all new, highly personalized, and completely true to our individual strengths. And most of it was psychological. It was about getting in the opponent's head, catching his rhythms, controlling his intention with subtle technical manipulation. When we went to Taiwan, we were ready for war.

CHAPTER 20

Taiwan

2004 Chung Hwa Cup
Tai Chi Chuan World Championships
Taipei, December 2–5, 2004

Clouds moved fast, dark and grey, the rain coming in gusts and then tapering off as Typhoon Nanmadol surged over the South China Sea. I've always loved storms; now these fierce winds made me electric. It was Thursday evening, forty hours from battle, and I stood at the peak of Elephant Mountain looking down on an Old Taoist Temple, the city of Taipei spread out below. The smell of incense wafted up from the temple shrine, smoke swirling in the building winds. I'd begun preparing for this tournament, the World Championships, the day after losing in the semifinals two years before. My last three months of training had been brutal. Night after night of pain, pushing myself to the absolute limit until nothing was left, and then dragging myself home to rest up for the next day's sessions. Now I stood, breathing deeply, soaking in the wind and rain. The sky to the west was a livid red—it was coming. I felt alive and ready.

* * *

There are two kinds of Push Hands in the Chung Hwa Cup. One is called Fixed Step. The other is Moving Step. Together they make up two divisions in this gigantic international competition that draws thousands of martial artists from more than fifty nations. The events are very different and most competitors specialize in either one or the other. It was my dream—in truth, it was my ambition—to win both.

The Moving Step game is fast, explosive, played in an eighteen-foot-diameter ring. The object is either to put your opponent on the ground or out of the ring. The inner game of Moving Step is subtle; it requires fine-tuned presence, technical mastery, and quickly evolving strategy. But from the outside much more apparent is the feral athleticism of the best fighters. It is a physical and mental melee of the highest order.

The Taiwan-style Fixed Step game is much more restrictive—in many ways, it is the truest test of a Tai Chi practitioner because there is no way to get around the internal principles of the art. There is no room to mask technical weakness with athleticism in Fixed Step. It is minimal, like haiku. You have two highly trained martial artists engaging in an explosive contest at very close range. There is great potential for injury because of violent clashing and sudden joint manipulation. The game is tight and the power generated is so condensed that an untrained spectator can often see nothing until one fighter suddenly goes flying away from the other and lands on his back eight or ten feet away.

Thursday night, about four hours after I got back from my blustery hike up Elephant Mountain, I found out that the tournament officials had changed the rules of the competition. Previous years in Taiwan, Fixed Step had been played on raised pedestals, each fighter standing with his right foot forward, left foot back about three feet to allow for a dynamic, rooted stance. In this year's competition, the Taiwanese removed the pedestals without any warning to foreign teams. This apparently small alteration in format would give a crucial advantage to the local teams who had been training under the correct conditions for the previous year. I will come back to this surprise soon—but first imagine a Fixed Step competition.

The forward feet of the opponents are lined up heel to toe, about one foot apart. Players are very close together, with opposing right wrists crossed and touching, and left hands hanging by the left hips like old Western gunfighters. In this posture the mental game begins. Players stand still, poised, vying for subtle advantages that will key explosive attacks. This moment is an energetic stare-down.

Then the ref says go and play erupts. The first to move a foot loses the point, or if someone is thrown to the ground, two points. If a lead ever exceeds ten points in a round, round over. At first glance, it looks like power and speed are decisive. Whoever is faster getting his hands on the other guy seems to win. But if you break the game down it becomes apparent that certain techniques refute other techniques. Every attack will get you thrown on the floor if met by the right counter, but moves and combinations of moves come so fast it feels like a guessing game—martial rock/paper/scissors.

This is only the beginning. There is a sea of potential that flows from this opening stance, an almost infinite number of feints, swift attacks from all angles, psychological ploys. In time, with years of creative training and a willingness to invest in loss, to take blow after blow and get blasted off the pedestals as a way of life, the game starts to slow down. You see attacks coming in slow motion and play refutational maneuvers in the blink of an eye. Great players are doing many invisible things in this game. It feels like chess. At the highest level of the sport, you are living inside your opponent's head and directing what he comes at you with.

Because each Fixed Step point begins exactly the same way, with two players assuming an identical opening posture, competitors can plan attacks in advance and over time build repertoires of combinations and defenses that they fire into when the ref sets play in motion—in the same manner that strong chess players have sophisticated opening repertoires. Since the first time I went to Taiwan four years earlier, I had been breaking down the game and creating Fixed Step theory that emerges from the agreed opening posture: standing on pedestals with the set hand positions. Taiwanese officials had sent us the exact dimensions of the pedestals months before this tournament. I had then internalized my arsenal of attacks and neutralizations, and was so comfortable with the game that I often trained with my eyes closed, allowing opponents to trigger first. My body would shrug off the attacks and explode into instinctual counters. All of this training was done while rooting on two small pedestals.

Now, one day before the competition begins, the news was that there were no pedestals and the rear hand would begin on the opponent's elbow instead of by the hip. This is a huge structural change. The equivalent in chess would be for a Grandmaster to spend five months preparing an opening repertoire for a World Championship match and then, before game one, to discover that the whole repertoire had been disallowed by a mysterious rule change.

In a minute everything had shifted, and we had a handful of hours to re-create an entire repertoire. On one level this was infuriating; on another it was predictable. Tai Chi is an emblem of Chinese and Taiwanese greatness. In a way, this discipline represents their sporting and philosophical essence. The top Taiwanese competitors train since childhood, many hours a day. If they win this tournament, they are national heroes. They take home a substantial cash prize and also get full scholarships to university. A career can be made in a day. Foreigners are welcome, but no one wants them to win. The Taiwanese pull out the stops to prevent it. It is a question of national pride.

At 1 A.M. Thursday night Max Chen and I were up exploring the nuances of this new structure. Max is my teacher's son and a very close friend of mine. He has been the U.S. National San Shou (Chinese kickboxing) Champion three times, and is an accomplished Push Hands player. Max knows what it's like to be on the front lines in international competition. We made a plan. Then I lay in bed visualizing until 3 A.M.

By Friday morning it was pouring torrentially. Typhoon Nanmadol was just offshore. I've been through a number of hurricanes on boats in the Bahamas, and something about this type of brooding, ominous buildup in the sky clicks me into a highly efficient place. I was on fire with ideas. We had intended to rest Friday, fill up the tanks, but that wasn't an option anymore with the new rules. The whole team, ten of us, gathered under a huge gazebo-type structure in the park by Hsinchuang Stadium, where the tournament would be held. After living and dying on the mats together for the past year, we were a family, a dedicated unit, with utter conviction about our work, and yet from one angle our situation was surely preposterous. We were gathered outside in a typhoon trying to figure out how to survive without pedestals. Max had spent the morning jogging through the downpour trying to sweat off four pounds before the weigh-in. The wind was howling and even under the gazebo, rain hit us horizontally.

Dan and I worked together refining new strategies on the fly. While our teammates did some light sparring, we spent two hours re-creating our Fixed Step theory. The key was to roll with the evolving situation and contour new tactics around the principles we had discovered back home. When hit with such surprises, if you have a solid foundation, you should be fine. Tactics come easy once principles are in the blood. I felt confident. House rules are almost always in effect when playing on the road—I knew this from the chess days and previous Taiwanese debacles. Handling dirty tricks is a part of the game.

DAY 1

Saturday morning. We arrived at the stadium and weighed in at 7:30 A.M., everybody hungry, but no eating until we made weight. After all the preparation, there is nothing like that feeling of icy reality that hits when the opening bell is near.

At the weigh station reality sunk in one step deeper when we saw Chen Ze-Cheng and his team—the dominant school in the world. He was the guy who had beaten me two years earlier and whom I had been preparing for all this time. I walked over and said hello, and Chen told me that he was competing under 75 kilos (165.3 pounds), the weight division below me. I was shocked. I had spent two years dreaming about this great fighter, strategizing against his sinuous cat-quick game; in my mind, winning the world championship had meant defeating Chen Ze-Cheng. But then he pointed toward their guy in my division and I took a deep breath. They called him Buffalo and he looked like pure power. In Taiwan he was considered unbeatable. He'd been groomed to become a world champion since he was a young boy. He was a little shorter than me and much thicker. He weighed in at 79.96 kilos (176.3 pounds). I weighed in at 78.16. He was four pounds heavier than me and probably cut fifteen pounds to make weight. The guy was a daunting physical specimen.

After the weigh-in, my team and I went and checked out the Moving Step ring. I felt the traction of the mats, then moved around a little. Immediately alarm bells were going off—the ring seemed too small. Tournament officials had sent us rules and ring dimensions months ago: a six-meter-diameter circle. We used their precise dimensions to set up our training mats for both Fixed and Moving. I had internalized the dimensions of the circle and knew exactly how it felt when my heel was a quarter inch from the edge. If you step over the border in Moving Step you lose a point, and in the flurries of action there is no time to look down—ring sense is hugely important. We measured and the diameter was fifteen inches smaller than what they had sent us. This was the second dirty trick and the matches hadn't even begun. So we had to adjust. Typical, but there was nothing to be gained by getting worked up about it.

We walked to the hotel in the rain, ate a big meal, and came back at 10 A.M. fueled for battle. The Fixed and Moving competitions would be going on at the same time. Two rings would be used for Moving Step, three for Fixed.

Weight divisions were every five kilos, with men and women competing separately. Over four thousand competitors from all over the world were milling around, and the stadium was mobbed with fans, many of them chanting euphonically in languages I didn't understand. It was a great, lilting, hypnotic sound. Acres away, on the far side of the arena, balletic Tai Chi form competition was taking place. Blood and meditation were coexisting.

My first match would be Moving Step. The rules, simply put, are as follows: Play begins from contact—this is a grappling competition like wrestling or judo, so striking is supposedly not encouraged. The target area is from the waist to just below the neck. You cannot lock your hands behind someone's back or grab their clothes, otherwise play is wide open. You gain one point for throwing the guy out of the ring, two points for a clean throw where the opponent hits the floor and you are standing. One point for a throw where you go down on top of the opponent. Matches are three rounds, two minutes playing time each. If someone leads by four points in a round, it is over. Two out of three rounds wins and if rounds and points are even by the end of three rounds, the lighter guy wins. That rarely happens, but if the Buffalo and I stayed healthy and managed to make it into the last round, it could give me a tiny edge.

My first Moving Step opponent was strong, fast, and aggressive. His speed surprised me—a very good athlete. All the players from the top Taiwanese schools have a way of putting the cardio load on the opponent and draining him with subtle pressure and leverage. They have excellent pummeling techniques, which means they know how to take inside position with their forward arm in the clinch. Imagine an opponent's left foot forward, left arm deep under my armpit and wrapped around my back or up my shoulder. That is an underhook. Pummeling is the fight for that position. The inside arm tends to give more leverage and slightly better angles for throws. If a player has "double inside position" it means that he has underhooks on both sides. This is considered to be very advantageous in all grappling arts. If you ever hear martial artists talking about a "pummeling war" they don't mean that two people are clobbering one another, but that they are fighting for underhooks.

It turns out that pummeling would be a huge component of my tournament strategy. You may recall that I hurt my right shoulder fighting Chen Ze-Cheng in the semifinals of the 2002 World Championships. Since then, the shoulder has been my Achilles heel. About three months before this year's Taiwan tournament, the 2004 Worlds, Dan came upon an interesting method in training. Whenever I had the right side underhook in the clinch, he would clamp down on my elbow from the outside in a manner that just killed my shoulder. After weeks of pain, I decided to concede the pummeling war and take double outside position in training to avoid damaging the shoulder any further. While I initially felt at a disadvantage giving Dan the underhooks, over time I became increasingly comfortable. I came up with some subtle ways to crimp his leverage and I found that I could make the angles work for me.

In my final ten weeks of preparation, when training with anyone other than Dan, I felt completely dominant from the outside position. My weakness had blossomed into a weapon that would prove critical for me in Taiwan. You see, the Taiwanese are lightning-quick with their pummeling and I made the decision early in the tournament not to fight it— don't play their game. By giving them that first position

241

they were so used to fighting for, I mitigated a large part of their training: the pummeling war. Then we would do battle in the setup I had become expert in, and that they hadn't studied as deeply. This happens all the time in chess at the highest levels; top players discover hidden resources in opening positions that had been considered theoretically weak. They become masters of a forgotten or undiscovered battleground and then guide opponents into the briar patch.

So my first opponent was very aggressive but nothing he brought felt dangerous. His pummeling was excellent and he came at me with tremendous confidence, but once I locked down on him from the outside his structure felt a little unsound, like a grand house with a flawed foundation. I knew that if I weathered his early attacks, I'd be fine. I crimped his attempts to use the underhooks and edged him out of the ring a couple of times. I went up two points in round one and just held the lead.

Then I watched the Buffalo. Wow! First he blew the other fighter out of the ring. Then, lightning-quick, he trapped both of the opponent's arms under his left armpit, took the guy's back, and flipped him over a deep leg. He manhandled the guy, and looked unbeatable. At one point after a throw it looked as if he would fall but he somehow did a full split, caught himself, with heel and toe, and just popped back up, getting the full two points. This was my man. I had to find a weakness but didn't see it.

My next match was Fixed Step. Not much problem, except for the judges. Many points that I won, the scorekeeper didn't record. This was infuriating but also hilarious. Imagine, the referee would signal that I'd won the point but the scorekeeper would neglect to write it down as if he'd forgotten or hadn't noticed. This happened again and again. My teammates and father were screaming about it, but nothing was done except that officials would nod to them with placid smiles. It happened to every foreigner in the tournament, sometimes decisively. This was the way they kept score here. Their country. Nothing to do but score more points and keep the static out of my head. Against most guys the judges couldn't really hurt me. But in the final rounds where we were evenly matched, there would be little margin for error. I tried not to think about it.

Whenever I had a break I watched the Buffalo. He won his points easily. He had fine technique but he was also much more powerful than his opponents. He could blast most guys right out of the ring in a flurry of explosive aggression. But I started to sense some small vulnerability. Maybe. He was technically sharp with dazzling footwork, speed, and a deeply rooted stance, but something about his structure teased me.

In my next Fixed Step match I faced off with the top guy from the school from Tainan that is the main rival to Chen Ze-Cheng's team. They are fierce competitors, like soldiers, strong, fast, well trained, pure aggression. All signs pointed to a war, but we touched hands and I knew I had him. You can read a lot about a martial artist from the opening contact. Great ones feel mountainous, like the earth is moving inside of them. Others ring more hollow. He bounced right off me on the first couple of points. Then I started mixing things up and he couldn't keep up with the tactics I threw at him. I won the first two rounds by a big margin, no injuries. Match over. I watched the Buffalo compete again in Fixed and he was overwhelming against a lesser opponent, but I had this building feeling that there was something a little wrong with his foundation. He was so physically gifted that it was easy to stand gaping as he tossed the guy to the floor left and right, but he seemed to be covering something up with all the flash. I wasn't sure why or how, but in Fixed he felt mortal. In Moving Step, he seemed unstoppable.

Day one was over and I wasn't injured. This is a long tournament, a marathon of sprints. Almost all of these martial arts competitions last only one day because players' bodies usually break down after that. You can push through virtually anything in eight or ten hours, but then the injuries burrow in overnight and you can't walk or lift your arms in the morning. This tournament is two days. You have to win on Saturday without getting badly hurt to have a chance to become World Champion on Sunday.

I went to bed listening to the rain outside my window, and I dreamed about the Buffalo.

DAY 2

Sunday morning, 8 A.M. We arrived at the stadium in time for an unhappy surprise. The Taiwanese officials had created a separate tournament for foreigners and scheduled to run it before the championship rounds. I was informed that participation was mandatory. I asked whether this could take place after the main event and was told that it was impossible. This absurd tournament within the tournament clearly had the function of exhausting and injuring foreigners who were still competing for medals against the Taiwanese in the Championship. A time-consuming protest ensued with a tremendous language barrier eventually being bridged by my teacher, who fortunately had some weight. It was agreed, finally, that those of us who were still in the main competition could take part after our final matches.

I had two fights left in each division to win. First was Moving semifinals, against the number one fighter from the tough Tainan school. Moving was his specialty and he came right at me, elbows tight in the pummeling, fast, persistent, putting the cardio load on me. He attacked early and I circled out but stepped on the line. My instincts were off—I thought I was well in bounds, but was wrong. On our mats at home I would have been in. Bad move. Down 1–0. We went back at it. I let him push me to the edge of the ring, baiting him, and exploded into a reversal that put him inches from the line, but he had a deep root and wouldn't go out. Then I switched gears and went on the offensive, pressuring him, using the Anaconda technique I had developed three months earlier—inching him out, surging, tightening the noose whenever he tried to squirm away, clamping down when he exhaled. In the final seconds I caught him with a beautiful throw but my shoulder got jammed on the landing.

I was on my back between rounds, breathing hard. This may have had a telling psychological effect. In preparation the last few months, we did a lot of interval training, building sprint time in the ring and working on recovery. We would play one-minute rounds with one-minute breaks between, sometimes going fifteen or twenty rounds like that, four of us playing, alternating play and recovery. My idea was to be able to have a wild sprint, drain myself completely, and know I could come back in the next round even if I felt like death baked over.

Interestingly, months before the competition the organizers told us that there would be thirty seconds between rounds and we found out upon arriving in Taiwan that it was one minute. So I had been doing this one-minute interval work with the team largely as a training mechanism to work on going all-out without overextending, and also to condense recovery time. Now we showed up and there were one-minute breaks between rounds. Their switch played right into our hands. I knew I could spend every last drop if I had to, and then I would be back and okay sixty seconds later if I lay on my back breathing deeply. I looked like a dead man between rounds, but was fine.

Round two. He shot right in at the bell. I held him off, gave him the underhooks, locked down, cranked, right, left, he went with it, but then I caught him on the third try, spun him out of the ring and onto the floor. These guys are great technicians and I really figured out how to shut them down. By just giving them that first position they were so used to fighting for, I created a new battlefield. There was no resistance where they expected it and then much more where they were less prepared. Amazing how it all started with an old shoulder injury.

I was in his head and up 2–0. He looked confused. Then the confusion turned to desperation and he charged me, putting everything he had into one last attack, torquing wildly, out of control. I went with the force, landed on my feet, and used the momentum to toss him out of the ring and onto the floor. Round and match were mine.

I watched the Buffalo annihilate another opponent. Just him and me in Moving Step for the title. I still didn't see a weakness in his game, but I had a plan. There were forty-five minutes before my Fixed Step semis and I had a rough time. My shoulder hurt so badly, I couldn't lift my right arm up past my waist. I was all banged up, black eye, forehead one big rug burn, pain all through me. The shoulder had me concerned. Dan and I were the only guys on our team left in the main draw and we sprawled on the mats while teammates massaged our legs, shoulders, arms. I put on my hood, sat in a corner, and hoped my body could hold out for three more matches; then it didn't matter.

They called me up for Fixed Step semis and it took a lot to walk over to the ring. My opponent was somebody I had been watching throughout the tournament—in his forties, barrel-chested, serene, and powerful, the man had the feeling of a samurai. He was older than almost all the competitors, the only guy his age still in the competition. I had watched him dispense with younger, athletic opponents left and right, and he clearly had amazing skill. What I didn't know is that he was one of the most respected teachers in the world. The stadium was loaded with his students. I heard chanting and knew it wasn't for me.

Round one. Our wrists connected and before the first point began he was working on me, taking space in that strange internal way some of these rare ones can. The ref said "Go!" I attacked fast, met empty space, and flew into it. Down 1–0. This guy had the stuff, the magic if there were magic in the martial arts. Next point I bounced off him. Powerful root. I couldn't attack him. I tried a lateral technique and won a point. He blasted me once and then pulled me into a black hole. I was down 4–1. I tend to feel pretty invincible in Fixed Step, but this man understood things about Tai Chi I had not yet discovered.

The rounds in Fixed Step are thirty seconds stop time (the clock is stopped after each point). This is enough time for 15–20 fast exchanges. Not much time to figure things out. I sank deep on an attack and actually moved him backward. My point, but a referee came over and said that the point didn't count because my opponent's initial structure was illegal. Strange logic. Then I scored another point that they waved off. I heard my team and pop going crazy.

I had been to this tournament twice before and both times was shocked by the mendacity of the judges. This time the pattern was familiar to me. Basically, this is how it works: There is grand ceremony welcoming the foreigners, but they don't want us to win. The way they tend to steer results is by making some horrific calls early in the match to get the momentum going in the direction of the local player. Usually when a foreign competitor starts to feel that the match is rigged he gets increasingly desperate and over-aggressive. Instead of competing with presence he becomes overwrought and caught up in a downward spiral. His game falls apart. Then, once the Taiwanese player is in control of the match, the judging becomes exceedingly fair. In fact, they become overly kind to create the illusion of fairness.

I knew all of this coming in. The key was to keep on winning points, and to immediately come back from a bad call with a huge surge. Don't get rattled! If I controlled the momentum of the game, it would be hard for judges to take matches away. That was the plan. To be honest, I also felt a lot of love for my opponent in this match. The whole stadium was against me, except for our U.S. contingent of ten. I didn't blame the Taiwanese for wanting their man to win.

I was down three points, and needed to come back. He won another one. I had to stop the slide now, right now, or I wouldn't be able to catch up. I'd created a move two months earlier that I thought might be decisive in the tournament. We called it the bear hug. I would allow my opponent to come straight in on my chest with a hard attack. My two arms circled fast behind him and on the push I sank deep while pulling him down with me. I could also crank left or right with it. When applied cleanly, it is disturbing to have this done to you because it feels like you're falling into a void and at the same time your wrist is exploding—no choice but to go down. I let him in, bear hug, put him on the floor—two points.

He was up 5–3 but hadn't ever seen the bear hug before. I used it again, and spun him right. Down 5–4. Now the judge came over and tried to mess with my head. He told me to adjust my left-hand position on the starting posture—just psychological manipulation. I smiled at the ref and kept fighting. Bear hug again, it's even. Now my opponent stepped off the mats and came back with a different feeling. He was beginning to understand. He changed his left arm to trap my right if I bear-hugged. He had answers and I had new variations. We were flowing now, moves coming fast like speed chess in Washington Square Park.

This Fixed Step game is a sublime experience. At first it feels fast and jolty, like a painful guessing game, but then the play slows down in your mind. Over the years, as I became more and more relaxed under this kind of fire, and as my body built up enough resistance that the blows didn't bother me, the game became completely mental. It almost always felt as though I was seeing or feeling the action in more frames than my opponents, and so I could zoom in on the tiniest details, like the blink of an eye or the beginning of an exhalation. When our wrists connected, I usually felt exactly what my opponent would come at me with, and I learned how to apply the subtlest of pressures in order to dictate his intention. But this great Fixed Step fighter imposed his own reality. I couldn't get in his head. Or every time I got in he kicked me back out.

I tried the bear hug again but he jammed it. He'd figured it out. My own teammates hadn't learned how to parry the bear hug in two months of work. This guy took seconds. I was down 7–5, without much time left in the round. I faked a hard attack, but then slipped in a right underhook and threw him away. I was down one point with 1.1 seconds left. I needed to score fast and surged hard with a four-strike combination that scored at the bell. Round one was a tie, barely.

The second round is always played with the left foot forward. For some reason my opponent's structure didn't feel quite as solid with the legs reversed in the opening position. I began sinking deeply on my attacks, playing with feints, tight combinations, and misdirection. I noticed that if I faked in my mind, without even moving, he felt it and responded. He was incredibly sensitive to intention, so I started unbalancing him with invisible attacks that I pulsed into but didn't actually manifest physically. I was getting in his head. He felt it and got aggressive, attacked hard, and blasted me away. But now I had him attacking, and I knew I had a deeper root. I started receiving his blows and bouncing him off—won a bunch of points. Then I made the mistake of coming straight in and he threw me on the floor—two points. If I lowered the sophistication of my game a hair, he destroyed me. He slipped into a zone and attacked hard. We were even with three seconds to go in the round. I uprooted him with a four-prong combination, most of which didn't actually happen. Then I took the next point at the bell with a huge surge and won the round.

Round three, right leg forward again, this was where he liked it, but me too. We started trading points, back and forth, a war. My team was chanting *Tiger, Tiger Buma Ye.*

(Bruce used to call me *Tiger* in the young chess days, and it stuck.) The rest of the crowd was chanting in Mandarin. They loved him, and I didn't blame them. Then I noticed a hole. He had found the solution to my bear hug, trapping my right forward elbow so I couldn't get outside of him—but if I flashed my mind to the bear hug, in jamming it he opened up his armpit to inside pummeling techniques. I started taking the underhook and tossing him left and right. Every point I was playing with invisible feints which he somehow felt, and then I exploited his reactions. Trippy idea. I was using his crazy perceptiveness against him. Finally I caught a throw where I got the right underhook and cranked him all the way over and around me. He hit the ground hard. In that moment I felt a wave of sorrow—like I killed the last unicorn. The match ended and we hugged. I told him he was an inspiration.

* * *

Fixed and Moving Step finals ahead, both against the Buffalo. We'd been measuring each other for the past two days. We both knew that this mammoth international competition would come down to our own little war. In Moving Step, he was a force of nature. He overwhelmed his opponents with bull rushes and highly evolved throws. His pummeling was incredible. Dan and I had broken his game down and saw that he integrated very precise trips and sweeps into most of his throws. I had to neutralize his footwork and power, not get steamrolled out of the ring, counterpunch, and look for holes. That was the plan.

There was a one-hour break before all the final matches. Fixed would be first, which was good—I'd seen a weakness in Buffalo's structure and was hoping to get in his head before the Moving. I was ready for war, listening to "Lose Yourself" on the headphones. I felt myself steeling against the world, like a freight train that just had its brakes cut.

FIXED STEP WORLD CHAMPIONSHIP FINALS

Buffalo walked toward the Fixed Step ring, stopped just short of me, looked me dead in the eyes, and screamed something primal, from the gut, one note. A chant called back from the bleachers and then the stadium exploded. This was their man. Our wrists touched and he was all aggression. Good. I had to use that. Keep him there. On the first point he surged into an attack that put me airborne. Then he came right back at me, but I let him in, circled around his elbows with my hands and sank deep. Bear hug. He went right down, two points. At the beginning of every exchange we stood right leg forward, the backs of our wrists connected, waiting for the ref's command to set play in motion. Those seconds of standoff are psychologically complex. You can calm an opponent or challenge his ego, make him lust for aggression. Over and over I lulled him forward with tiny little openings. He was like a bull seeing red, charging in hard and fast, and I was always gone before he connected. I won two points that the ref waved off. I heard people grumbling about the officiating, but at this point I didn't care. I was a bit of a madman, deep in the zone. I knew that the only way to win was to win big. The bear hug was deadly against Buffalo's power. He kept on hitting the floor and seemed confused. Round one was a blowout.

In round two I felt unstoppable. I didn't care about the refs or the score. I kept winning one point after the next after

the next and I heard Dan and my teammates chanting *Tiger,*
Buma Ye, Tiger, Buma Ye. I was in his head and kept on
coming. My father said this was his favorite match, that it
was a beautiful, emotional experience to watch. To me it felt
technical: I won it before stepping in the ring. Afterward my
team mobbed me and Max lifted me into the air. The stadium was silent but for the voice of my pop and the guys
around me. I was World Champion.

Now let's see if I could do it twice.

MOVING STEP FINALS

Buffalo entered the ring screaming, wild, fists pumping
the air. I had felt his mortality in Fixed, which was good,
but the Moving Step would be his legacy. He'd trained his
whole life to be World Champion. I had no solutions to his
game, only ideas. He was surely the greater athlete. But
maybe I was the better thinker. The bell rang and he went
right on the attack, pummeling in for the underhooks. For
a few seconds I fought for the inside position but he felt too
powerful and I decided to give it to him—no reason to
meet him head-on. His left arm pummeled deep under my
right armpit and wrapped up my shoulder. My right foot
was forward and my right arm locked down on his left
upper arm. He had better leverage for edging me out and for
certain throws, but I had some excellent weapons as well.
When the timing felt right I cranked to the left. We went
down hard together. I instigated the throw, but my left
elbow touched just before he crashed down. His point, 1–0.
My shirt was ripped up; I didn't mind the cave man feeling,
but the officials made me change it.

I'd lost the first point but felt potential. Play resumed, we connected, I disconnected, then came straight in on him and tried to jump around and take his back but he was too quick and wrapped me up. We separated, I danced around him, tried to enter fast and spin him but nothing there. We felt each other out. Then he cranked hard, I went with it, spun with the force and stayed on my feet, but when I landed he was on me, pushing hard. I rooted it out, but he kept on coming, relentless, and he edged me out of the ring. I'm down 2–0. About a minute to go in round one. I tried a couple of things but couldn't find a hole. He was confident, too strong; I needed to use that strength, there was nothing else. I went into the clinch and leaned on him, let him feel my weight and also my exhaustion. He started to edge me out of the ring, and I let him take me there. He was cautious, tiny steps, no overextension. My back was to the edge, I planted my left foot an inch from the line, and exploded, drove hard against his right arm, screaming, putting everything I had into this throw. He couldn't hold on and I took him out of the ring and then went down hard on top of him. It's 2–1, eleven seconds left in the round. I needed a point and was tapped out. Dan was screaming, my whole team was chanting, *Tiger, Tiger Buma Ye,* faster and faster. *I need to go buck wild now, need one point, gotta let it all hang out.* The ref said "Go!" and I hit him like a truck, he gave a little, then held his ground, trying to hold on for the bell. I cranked and we started spinning, my back to the edge, then his, then mine again, total chaos. I screamed as I pulled hard and reversed him. He was on the edge but had the underhooks, was okay, incredible root, and then all I can say is that I reached deeper than I knew I had and won the most dramatic point of my life. With one second left I drove him out of the ring, launching through him and over him, landing him on his back, my shoulder into his and my head over him straight into the ground. The bell rang, the crowd went totally wild, even the Taiwanese; 2–2.

I had sixty seconds and was a dead man. I lay panting on my back for almost all of that time. On the video, Buffalo looks physically strong but upset. Max rubbed my shoulders, I slowed down my breathing, thought I'd be okay by the bell. Hoped. Wasn't so sure.

Round two. He entered the ring like an enraged beast and the bleachers erupted in chants. I remember getting to my feet and walking slowly to the center, hoping I could reach it without falling over. He attacked immediately and the force went through me, into the ground. It felt like an electric current and I bounced him off, awake now, ready to roll. No more pain. He came at me again and cranked hard into a throw while sweeping out my right foot, but I felt it coming, stepped up with my left, and neutralized it while crimping his arms. I knew I had to watch that footwork, very dangerous. We went back into the clinch. I gave him the left underhook and clamped down on the arm. He probed for a hole and I held him off, waiting, listening; the game had grown smaller now, everything slowing down. He switched his weight into his front leg to attack and I caught it, fired into a throw in that flash that he was stuck, his foot entering the ground, no way to move, and he went down with me right on top, my shoulder into his left side. Up 1–0. He came right back at me, shaking off the last moment with a bull rush, but I felt it coming and went with the force, pulled him a little farther and he hit the ground. Up 2–0. Then I pulled off another throw, catching the same hole in his footwork, perfect timing, inner reap, we both went up and I landed on him hard. I'm up 3–0!

Now I made my only real mistake of the tournament. I had him totally defeated, he came at me, and I popped him to the side, his left foot landing inches from the edge. Then I should have backed off or gone in slow, but I smelled the finish line and charged, overextended, and he put me down. Two points, 3–2, he's back in it. My mistake. Not much time left. I'm spent, so is he. Here things really started to go out of control. He surged right at me. I used the force and almost put him down but he barely saved himself. We flew all over the place, him attacking, me neutralizing, counterattacking, him saving. I heard Max scream "Josh! Fifteen seconds!" I put a huge effort into a throw that he barely stopped. He charged, I warded it off, and I was exhausted; it felt like the fifteen seconds were over. Now, two years later, I see on the video—Max is waving at the timekeeper, the woman is standing holding the bell. What happened here was surreal. There were many witnesses, all with the same story. The clock hit 2:00 and the woman went to hit the bell but an official motioned for her not to ring it. Clock went to 2:04, :05, :06, we were scrambling in the ring, in total mayhem. I'd paced myself to last fifteen seconds and now I was way past blown out. I was up 3–2 and they were holding the bell. Everyone was screaming. I was dead on my feet, and the Buffalo put his heart, soul, blood, and guts into one more throw. I couldn't hold it off and started to go; he piled down on top of me, won the point, and they rang the bell, 3–3.

Officially the first two rounds were tied. I was on my back, slowing down my breathing, far beyond the most exhausted I'd ever been. Max and Dan rubbed my arms and shoulders. The bell rang. Round three, it all comes down to this. I had the tie-break if we were even. At this point it is pure guts. Survival. You operate on another plane of reality, second to second, relying on your training to keep you standing. The round began and I held him off, then gave up the double underhooks and launched into a throw I've been working on for years and hadn't shown yet at the tournament. I trapped his right arm under my left elbow, pulsed forward to provoke a reaction, and then turned left, rolling over my right shoulder and his trapped right arm, all my weight pulling down and away from his root. He flew over me in a big circle and we went down hard, my shoulder into his ribs. Perfectly executed, but the judges didn't give it to me. I was too tired to be angry about it. They said we touched the floor at the same time. His ribs wouldn't agree. No score. I didn't have much left. We felt each other out for ten seconds, then he attacked, forced a lean, and spun me on the mat, lovely throw. I'm down 2–0. *Trouble. Gotta dig deep. Find something.*

Now he changed tactics and decided to hold me off, stalling out the round. I searched for over a minute, spent; on the video it looks like I gave up. My body went limp, then I saw a hole and exploded into the same throw they just took away from me, but at the end I pushed off hard (incidentally against my ankle, which was turned ninety degrees), arched my back, and landed flat on him so they couldn't argue. My point, 2–1. *Need one more from somewhere.*

It felt like one of those video games where the endurance of the fighter is gone and you have to hold the other guy off, survive the barrage, until you've recovered enough to give him one more shot. That's what I had to do, hold him off until I had a little bit in me, and then put every ounce of it into a throw that had to be perfectly timed because if it didn't work I might just collapse.

Then I found a little opening. I got into the clinch, trapped his right arm, faked forward, and drove my whole being into a bicep throw. He went down, I landed on him, shoulder to ribs. The tying point. There were nineteen seconds left. *All I have to do is hold him off and I win.* Except at this moment everything turned very, very strange. Once again, the judges decided not to allow my throw. They claimed it was illegal. Now people rushed onto the floor, Americans and Taiwanese officials. Our team had cameras shooting the match and soon a gaggle of officials and players from both teams were looking into video cameras. The stadium went berserk with anger and confusion. The judges convened, the president of the Taiwanese federation, my teacher Master Chen, my whole team, my opponent's team, everyone on the mats looking at the videos. There were fifteen minutes of mayhem, bickering, politics.

Interestingly, my opponent's coach and his whole team considered the ruling against me an outrage—they told me this afterward. By all accounts my throw was legal. It was astonishing that hometown referees would do this in the final minute of a match for the world title. After a long dispute, the judges said this challenge would have to be resolved after the match. But for now, I was down by one, the throw would not be counted, and there were 19 seconds left. I had to continue or I would lose by forfeit. Well, in those 19 seconds I gave it my all. I attacked him with everything I had, made the situation totally chaotic and cranked into a throw that would have put him down in training, but he gave up his body, literally. His elbow bent all the way back; it was exploding inside, but he wouldn't give up and stayed on his feet until the bell rang. Such heart!

Then I just sat down and watched chaos take over. Witnesses came from all over who had seen the clock run out in round two when the judge had refused to allow the woman to ring the bell. There was a meeting held in the center of the stadium with videos shown to the president of the Taiwanese Tai Chi Federation, to the judges, to everybody. My opponent's coach, Chen Ze-Cheng's father, an honorable man, agreed with the president that this was wrong. They suggested a shared championship. I went over to the head referee and demanded a clear winner. Overtime. I knew I could take him. The opposing coach agreed to a two-minute sudden death playoff to decide the World Championship. We would have international judges. They went to find the Buffalo. For twenty minutes I paced the arena, red hot—if there is a place beyond the zone, I was there. But it turned out that Buffalo's elbow was too severely injured. The ruling was a shared title in Moving Step. In a flash, it was over. No more battles to fight. The martial fury subsided, and in its place came pain, mellowness and camaraderie. Buffalo and I swayed on the first place podium together, hugging, and holding each other up.

AFTERWORD

Two years after the madness of that World Championship in Taiwan, I am still digesting the experience. Never in my life have I had to dig so deeply into myself. Not even close. It was thrilling and also a bit alienating. I saw parts of myself I didn't know about. To survive and win, I became a gladiator, pure and simple. I hadn't fully understood that he was inside of me, waiting, but surely all the work I had done for years had made him possible, perhaps inevitable.

How did this new part of myself relate to the Josh I'd known my whole life, the kid who was once scared of the dark, the chess player, the young man who loves the rain and re-reading passages of Jack Kerouac? How did it fit in with my passion for Buddhism and the satyagraha of Mahatma Gandhi? Honestly, these are questions that I am still sorting out. Do I want to explore more of this side of myself? Maybe. But perhaps in a different guise. Mainly what I felt after Taiwan was an urgent desire to get back to practice and shake off the idea that I had climbed my mountain. In the last two years I have started over. A new beginning. There are great adventures ahead.

* * *

The writing off this book has spanned an intense and unlikely stretch of years. As a kid growing up, in my tiny room I could never have dreamed that such battles awaited me. While writing these pages, my ideas have evolved, loves have fallen apart and come anew, world championships were lost and won. If I have learned anything over my first twenty-nine years, it is that we cannot calculate our important contests, adventures, and great loves to the end. The only thing we can really count on is getting surprised. No matter how much preparation we do, in the real tests of our lives, we'll be in unfamiliar terrain. Conditions might not be calm or reasonable. It may feel as though the whole world is stacked against us. This is when we have to perform better than we ever conceived of performing. I believe the key is to have prepared in a manner that allows for inspiration, to have laid the foundation for us to create under the wildest pressures we ever imagined.

It is my hope that you, the reader, emerge from this book inspired and perhaps a bit more enabled to follow your dreams in a manner that is consistent with the unique gifts you bring to the table. That has been my ambition. The ideas I've shared in these pages have worked for me and it's my hope that they suggest a structure and direction. But there is no such thing as a fixed recipe for victory or happiness. If my approach feels right, take it, hone it, give it your own flavor. Leave my numbers behind. In the end, mastery involves discovering the most resonant information and integrating it so deeply and fully it disappears and allows us to fly free.

ACKNOWLEDGEMENTS

My father, Freddy Waitzkin, has had my back through it all. Pop, I can't thank you enough for all the love, patience, guidance, and loyalty. You've been in my corner through thick and thin, and we both know I couldn't have done it without you. Mom, you're the greatest mother anyone could ever dream of. Katya, my gutsy dive partner and baby sister, I am so proud of you. I love you guys. In our crazy Waitzkin way, we keep it together.

I've been blessed with some wonderful teachers in my life. My Grandma, Stella Waitzkin, whom I miss terribly, taught me to listen. Shellie Sclan got me writing. Dennis Dalton and Robert Thurman got me feeling. William C. C. Chen taught me to let go. John Machado has me rolling all over again.

My dear friends and teammates, Dan Caulfield, Max Chen, Tom Otterness, Jan C. Childress, Jan L. Childress, Trevor Cohen, and the Little Warrior: Irving Yee—thank you, guys, for helping me create our laboratory. We've got a long way to go.

As for the birth of this book, I am enormously indebted to my agent Binky Urban, who was just plain great. Thank you so much for your patience and your vision, Binky.

My fabulous editor Liz Stein believed in this book from

day one and then gave me the room to bring it together. It is a true pleasure working with you, Liz, and I have learned so much from the process.

Mike Bryan, John Maroon, and John Henrich, many thanks for reaching out with such generosity.

I had some readers who gave me valuable feedback when I needed it. Desiree Cifre, Bonnie Waitzkin, Elta Smith, Bindu Suresh, Hannah Beth King, Toby Buggiani, Tom Otterness, Dan Caulfield, you guys are great. Pop, you've been a rock.

Light Buggiani, David Arnett, Rebecca Mayer, Maurice Ashley, Andy Manning, Jeffrey Newman, Mike Bryan, Paul Pines, Carol Jarecki, Bruce Pandolfini, Svetozar Jovanovic, Diana and Jonathan Wade, thank you for the friendship and inspiration.

Desi baby, you are a dream come true.

ABOUT THE AUTHOR

Josh Waitzkin, an eight-time National Chess Champion in his youth, was the subject of the book and movie *Searching for Bobby Fischer*. At eighteen, he published his first book, *Josh Waitzkin's Attacking Chess*. Since the age of twenty, he has developed and been spokesperson for Chessmaster, the largest computer chess program in the world, currently in its eleventh edition. Now a martial arts champion, he holds a combined twenty-one National Championship titles in addition to several World Championship titles. He regularly gives seminars and keynote presentations and is president of the JW Foundation, a nonprofit devoted to maximizing each student's unique potential through an enriched educational process.